SO-BBT-125

64 Yard & Garden PROJECTS

You Can Build Yourself

Monte Burch

WITHDRAWN

A Storey Publishing Book

STOREY

STOREY COMMUNICATIONS, INC.
SCHOOLHOUSE ROAD
POWNAL, VERMONT 05261

SCHAUMBURG TOWNSHIP DISTRICT LIBRARY
32 WEST LIBRARY LANE
SCHAUMBURG, ILLINOIS 60194

684.08
BUR

3 1257 01004 9285

Edited by Deborah Balmuth and John Matthews, Wood-Matthews Editorial Services, Inc.

Cover design by Greg Imhoff

Cover illustrations by Brigita Fuhrmann

Text design and production by Cindy McFarland

Production assistance by Susan Bernier

Interior Photographs by Monte Burch

Line drawings by Monte Burch

Indexed by Northwind Editorial Services

Copyright © 1994 by Monte Burch

All rights reserved. No part of this book may be reproduced without written permission from the publisher, except by a reviewer who may quote brief passages or reproduce illustrations in a review with appropriate credits; nor may any part of this book be reproduced, stored in a retrieval system, or transmitted in any form or by any means — electronic, mechanical, photocopying, recording, or other — without written permission from the publisher.

The information in this book is true and complete to the best of our knowledge. All recommendations are made without guarantee on the part of the author or Storey Communications, Inc. The author and publisher disclaim any liability in connection with the use of this information. For additional information please contact Storey Communications, Inc., Schoolhouse Road, Pownal, Vermont 05261.

Printed in the United States by Book Press

First Printing, October 1994

Library of Congress Cataloging-in-Publication Data

Burch, Monte.
    64 yard and garden projects you can build yourself / Monte Burch.
    p. cm.
    Includes index.
    ISBN 0-88266-834-X — ISBN 0-88266-846-3 (pbk.)
    1. Woodwork. 2. Garden ornaments and furniture. 3. Gardening — Equipment and supplies. I. Title.
    TT180.B83 1994
    684'.08—dc20   94-13330
                                          CIP

CONTENTS

Preface

I DESIGNED THE PROJECTS in this book to do several things. First, I wanted to make gardening chores less of a hassle by cutting down on the amount of hard work like weeding, carrying, stooping, and bending. Second, I wanted these projects to provide you with more leisure time in your garden. Third, I wanted to include projects that would be enjoyable to look at and might become a special addition to your garden or backyard landscaping scheme. Lastly, I wanted these garden projects to be both fun to build and something to take pride in. Whether you're a gardener looking for something useful to make or a woodworker who likes to garden, you should be able to find something here.

When the pole bean tower was erected in my garden, it prompted a lot of curiosity — and a few jokes — from my neighbors. But I made it quickly and it worked beautifully! Most of the projects in this book are not complicated, and some are even a little "rough." Most projects don't require a great deal of experience, and you can make most of them somewhere between an hour and a Sat-

urday afternoon. And simple, rewarding projects sure beat the couch potato routine!

I've also included a few larger projects such as a garden shed and a couple of greenhouses. The garden shed and one greenhouse are even portable — you can place them where they are most useful and take them with you when you move.

Even the big projects, however, aren't too complicated. I've tried to provide as much assistance as I can by helping you choose the right tools, learn how to use those tools, and put together each project by taking you through each step of construction. While some designs are certainly more complicated than others — like the around-the-tree bench — most are straightforward to build and are good places for beginners to learn basic woodworking skills. On the other hand, skilled woodworkers won't be bored, either.

The designs in this book fall into several categories: porch, patio, deck, and indoor projects; garden projects; greenhouses and greenhouse-accessory projects; projects for the yard; and fencing for the garden and yard.

These categories are rough — you are as likely to use the movable work center in your garden as in your yard — so don't be afraid to browse through all of the sections for something you'd like to make.

I've always involved my family in books and building projects and this book was no exception. My son Michael spent the summer helping with construction; my daughter Jodi sanded, painted, and stained; and Mom ran the show. Your family can also join in to build these projects. Many of the simple projects are a good place to turn youngsters loose with a hammer and saw.

Usually we grow a huge garden, and we did this year as well. Unfortunately, we spent most of our time constructing and designing these projects and too little time gardening. But I look forward to enjoying my garden and my garden projects more next year. I hope you get as much fun and enjoyment out of using these projects as we plan to!

Materials

AFTER GOING THROUGH all the time and expense of building your garden projects, you'll want them to last and provide good service, which means you should use durable materials. This chapter will help you learn about finding and using quality materials for making quality projects.

Wood

The majority of the projects are constructed primarily of wood, so selecting the proper wood is extremely important. The types of wood most commonly used in outdoor projects are pressure-treated lumber, California redwood, and western red cedar, which are all long lasting and decay and insect resistant. The latter two are the most expensive but are often chosen where appearance is important. There are many other less-common species available, too.

It is important to remember that although kiln-dried dimension lumber is cut to its nominal dimension at the mill, the dimensions are

Choosing the correct materials for an outdoor project is extremely important in order for the project to be durable. The materials should also suit the project's purpose. For small decorative pieces that will be used on a patio, deck, or porch and where cost isn't as important as the finish, redwood and western cedar are good choices.

smaller after drying and planing. For example, 2×4s actually measure about 1½ inches by 3½ inches, 2×6s measure 1½ inches by 5½ inches, 2×8s are actually 1½ inches by 7¼ inches, and 2×10s are often 1½ inches by 9¼ inches. It's important to measure the actual lumber at hand. Some 2×4s might be 3½ inches wide, some 3¼, and some 3⅜.

Rot-Resistant Species

The United States Forest Products Laboratory classes redwood heartwood among a limited number of American woods that are durable even when used under conditions that favor decay. Redwood has been successfully employed for exterior siding, stadium seats, silos, tanks, bridges, trestles, and almost any other exterior structure that requires a serviceable, long-lasting wood.

One outstanding quality of redwood that makes it desirable for both outdoor and interior uses is its low rate of shrinkage and swelling under variable humidity levels. In other words, when redwood is used outside and is exposed to rain one day and sunshine the next, it stays in place well with little if any tendency to warp or split. It also has good nail-holding ability. And the texture of redwood is uniform and the grain straight. These characteristics permit you to work a smooth surface in fine detail. Finally, redwood contains no pitch or resins and, with its open cellular structure, properly dried redwood will retain paints

---

POLE BUILDING

Some of the projects in this book utilize pole-building methods. This is a very simple, fast, effective, and economical method of constructing a wide variety of projects. It consists of anchoring poles or posts in the ground and then constructing the project on the posts or poles. It's quick and inexpensive because no foundation or concrete is required for a floor. The depth the posts must be embedded depends on the local weather and geographic conditions. A check with local building supply dealers or better yet your county Extension agent will reveal the depth and size poles and posts you'll need for your area.

The posts are held in the ground in one of several different fashions: tamped earth, concrete punch pads, butt encasement, and full encasement. The latter two techniques are used primarily for larger barns and buildings; tamped earth and concrete punch pads will suffice for the smaller projects in this book. For more detailed information on pole building, you might be interested in *Monte Burch's Pole Building Projects* available from Storey/Garden Way Publishing.

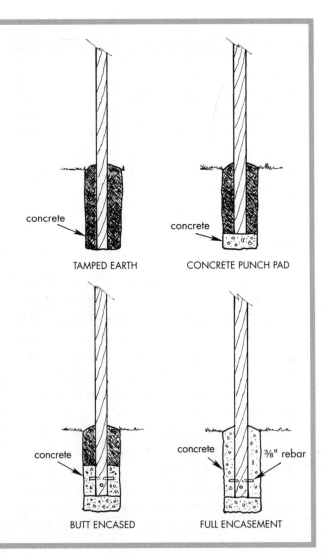

concrete — TAMPED EARTH

concrete — CONCRETE PUNCH PAD

concrete — BUTT ENCASED

concrete — ⅜" rebar — FULL ENCASEMENT

---

or other finishes longer than most other woods. It is a natural choice in the garden.

Redwood is available in several grades with the seven most popular being clear all-heart, clear, select heart, select, construction heart, construction, and merchantable. Excellence of appearance, clearness, and freedom from knots are the determinants for the highest grades. Middle and lower grades are categorized by the number, size, and nature of knots and other characteristics each piece contains. For determining durability against termite and decay attack, redwood is graded by color. The reddish-brown heartwood from the inner portion of the tree contains colored extractives that render it durable. The cream-colored sapwood or alburnum from the outer growth layer of the trees, like most whitewood species, does not possess the heartwood's resistance to decay and termites.

The construction grades are perfectly fine for garden projects. Construction heart is a good general-purpose grade that is economical and suitable for most of these projects. It is excellent for posts, decking, retaining walls, fences, and garden structures. Construction grade contains more sapwood and is used for fencing and aboveground rough construction that does not require the exceptional durability of the all-heartwood grades.

Several other types of wood are also long lasting and attractive. Cedar is an extremely good choice. Western white cedar is one obvious choice, but cedar is also available in many areas as aromatic red cedar, the familiar wood used for cedar blocks, cedar chests, and closet linings. Slow growing and naturally durable, western red cedar has one of the longest lifespans of any North American softwood and is an excellent material. Western red cedar's most valuable characteristic is its well-known resistance to decay, which comes from the presence of naturally occurring fungicidal compounds in the wood called thujaplicins.

Finish isn't as important on such larger projects as fences. Pressure-treated lumber is fast becoming the most popular outdoor building material across the nation. Pressure-treated lumber is readily accessible, fairly economical and extremely long lasting.

Another extractive present in the wood, thujic acid, helps make the wood resistant to insect attack.

If exposed for prolonged periods to conditions where decay could be a factor, such as where the wood is in contact with the ground,

cedar should be treated with suitable wood preservatives. But when properly finished and maintained, cedar will deliver decades of trouble-free service.

It is important to remember when using western red cedar that this species has a corrosive effect on some unprotected metals, causing a black stain on the wood. Fasteners should be made of a corrosion-resistant material such as aluminum, brass, or hot-dipped galvanized or stainless steel.

Other cedar species you may find helpful as alternatives include eastern red cedar, northern white cedar, and Atlantic white cedar. All are excellent choices.

Several other popular outdoor building woods are regionalized or available from local sawmills, although some are easier to work with than others. Most are milled and used green (uncured), which may cause splitting and other problems in the more intricate projects. Used as poles for grape trellises or fences, they're perfectly fine. Ask your local miller or building supply dealer if you have questions. Good "exotic" choices in the Northeast are black cherry and tamarack. In the South, cypress is an excellent material. Osage orange (sometimes called hedgeapple or bodark) is found throughout the Midwest, West, and Southwest and will outlast more than one generation of farmer. If you have wood and can get it milled for less than commercially produced lumber, you're ahead of the game. But usually the cost of the milled lumber is higher, even if you furnish it yourself. For posts and poles, however, you can simply cut your own wood with a chainsaw.

Unfortunately, it is also important to keep in mind that redwood, the cedars, cypress, and other naturally rot-resistant species have been heavily harvested. Commercial sources of these woods are often very expensive, which is a factor in the decline of supplies. Some of these species might even become endangered from irresponsible cutting, particularly in the case of redwood since heartwood

SAFETY PRECAUTIONS WITH PRESSURE-TREATED WOOD

→ Dispose of treated wood by ordinary trash collection or burial. Treated wood should not be burned in open fires or in stoves, fireplaces, or residential boilers because toxic chemicals may be produced as part of the smoke or ashes.

→ Avoid prolonged or frequent inhalation of sawdust from treated wood. When sawing and machining treated wood, wear a dust mask.

→ Whenever possible, sawing and machining should be performed outdoors to avoid indoor accumulation of airborne sawdust from treated wood.

→ When power-sawing and machining, wear goggles to protect eyes from flying particles.

→ After working with treated wood and before eating, drinking, and using tobacco products, wash exposed areas thoroughly.

→ If preservatives or sawdust accumulate on clothing, launder before reuse. Wash work clothes separately from other household clothing.

→ Do not use treated materials if the preservative may become a component of human or animal food, as with containers for storing grain. Treated wood should also not be used for cutting boards or countertops.

lumber often comes from old-growth forests. If you decide to use any of these wood species, remember to do so responsibly so future woodworkers also have the option to use them.

Pressure-Treated Wood

Pressure-treated wood has quickly become the most popular outdoor and garden building wood choice for several reasons. Pressure-treated wood is the most readily available outdoor building material throughout the country and comes in a wide range of sizes and types, even in the form of plywood. Many projects such as decks have been designed to show off the grayish natural color of the unfinished pressure-treated wood. Probably its single most important facet, however, is its relatively economical cost.

All pressure-treated woods are not alike. Since pressure-treated wood is available from many dealers and is manufactured by many national and regional companies, I suggest that you purchase only brand-name wood such as Wolmanized pressure-treated wood products available from the Hickson Corporation. Most national brands carry a lifetime limited warranty, which means the warranty is good from the date of purchase for as long as you own the property on which your stationary projects are built or as long as you own your movable projects. Look for an identifying label and/or stamp on the wood. Regardless of the brand chosen, the label or stamp should indicate approval by the American Wood Preservative Bureau. Remember as well to choose a grade appropriate to your use, since some pressure-treated woods are only for aboveground use while others can be buried or withstand submerged freshwater contact.

Wolmanized wood is treated under pressure with preservatives. There are three main types: chromated copper arsenate (CCA), ammoniacal copper arsenate (ACA), and ammoniacal copper zinc arsenate (ACZA).

In the case of CCA-treated wood, the preservative ingredients become fixed in the wood cells as leach-resistant, insoluble precipitates of copper arsenate and chrome arsenate, which do not vaporize or evaporate.

Is pressure-treated wood safe to use? At this writing, there is no simple or definitive answer to that question that can be applied across all situations. The answer partially depends on how you plan to use the treated wood. There is widespread agreement, for instance, that treated wood should not be put in places where it might come into contact with food, as with cutting boards or silos. On the other hand, there is disagreement among researchers about whether or not treated wood is acceptable to use for raised garden beds. Some fear that toxic chemicals will leach from the treated boards into the garden, but there is little consensus about what if anything actually does leach out and what might or might not be safe levels of specific chemicals. Right now, treated wood is used very widely and is generally accepted without question. You will see in the photographs of this book that I have extensively employed treated wood. However, if you feel unsure about the safety of treated wood, I recommend that you seek out reliable local sources for the latest information. County Extension agents, garden clubs, garden supply centers, building supply centers, and gardening magazines all might have up-to-date answers to your questions. Be aware that this debate will continue and probably won't be resolved quickly or completely for some time.

Finishes

Naturally, in most instances you'll desire to apply a finish to the projects in this book, although you may prefer to allow some to simply weather to a soft gray, particularly those made of treated wood, cypress, or redwood.

A wide variety of finishes can be used, including oil sealers, sealer/stains, varnishes,

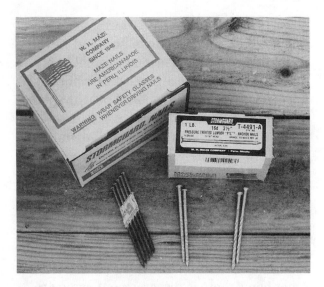

All fasteners should be rustproof. Hot-dipped galvanized zinc nails are the first choice in most cases. Some fasteners, such as these ITW Paslode nails and Stormguard PTL nails, are made for use specifically with pressure-treated lumber.

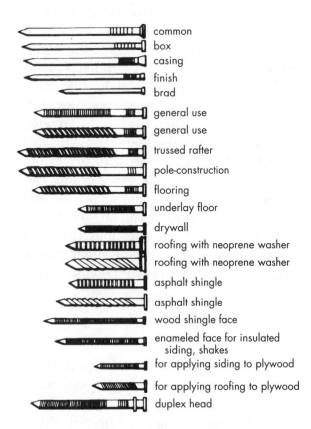

common
box
casing
finish
brad
general use
general use
trussed rafter
pole-construction
flooring
underlay floor
drywall
roofing with neoprene washer
roofing with neoprene washer
asphalt shingle
asphalt shingle
wood shingle face
enameled face for insulated
    siding, shakes
for applying siding to plywood
for applying roofing to plywood
duplex head

Sometimes it's hard to know what a particular nail looks like or what it's for. This illustration should help.

and paints. Make sure you read the instructions with the materials to determine that they are for exterior projects. Either latex- or oil-based paints can be used, although an oil stain is often longer lasting and easier to apply.

Do *not* use paint containing lead on livestock equipment or on parts of buildings accessible to livestock. Poisoning may result when animals constantly lick or chew objects covered with paint containing lead.

If you prefer the appearance of natural wood colors for some of the projects, boiled linseed oil is an excellent preservative and adds plenty of protection. It is nontoxic to livestock; can be brushed, rolled, or sprayed on; and is fairly economical. These days a wide variety of specialty penetrating oil finishes are available that provide even more protection. Some penetrating oil finishes are also formulated specifically for use with treated woods and will provide even more protection. They usually prevent the minute checking and cracking that occurs when the treated wood dries out and shrinks.

Fasteners

Several different types of fasteners will be used for these outdoor garden projects. Using the proper size and kind of fastener for the job adds to the project's longevity, ease of construction, and final appearance. Regardless of the type of fastener you use, coated fasteners should be your choice for outdoor projects.

Nails

Nails are sold by the pound or in prepackaged boxes. Bulk nails are cheaper but are usually only sold by lumber yards and building supply dealers. The larger chain building supply dealers sell only the boxed versions because boxes don't require someone to weigh and sack nails for customers. Nails come in a wide variety of sizes and styles. They are measured by the "penny" (abbreviated *d*). An "eight-penny" or 8d nail is about 2½ inches long, whereas a 10d nail is 3 inches long. The nails used most often are 4d, 6d, 8d, and 16d.

Several different types of nails are also available such as common nails, which have a large flat head, and finish (or finishing) nails, which have a smaller head that is set below the wood surface for a more finished appearance. Brads are tiny nails.

Nails are also available with or without protective coatings. If they are to be exposed to weather and moisture, they should be coated with galvanizing or zinc. If uncoated, plain steel nails are used they will rust, cause unsightly streaks and wood discoloration, and have a shorter life. Hot-dipped zinc-coated nails are the most common type found in outdoor projects as they're fairly economical and readily available.

You'll need special hardware and other items for projects such as this decorative gate.

Screws

Screws are also available in a wide range of sizes that are denoted by a number and a length, such as #8 2-inch screws. The smaller the first number, the smaller the screw. Screws are either plain steel, coated, or brass, with the latter two the best choice for exterior projects. Screws may have flat or round heads. The flat heads are normally countersunk below the wood surface, while round heads protrude. The screw head may also have a single slot or two crossed slots (Phillips) for tightening, with a Phillips head better for most outdoor projects.

Lag Screws

Lag screws are large screws with a hexagonal head without any slots. A wrench can be fitted over the head to tighten the screw. They're excellent for fastening heavy exterior projects.

Bolts

Bolts are also often used in fastening together some outdoor projects. They should always be used with washers as the pressure of fastening them together will force the heads and nuts into the wood surface.

Hardware

Butt hinges are specified in several projects. They are simply two leaf hinges fastened together with a pin. They are available in many sizes and in either steel or brass.

Angle irons are a very common hardware item. They are steel braces shaped in an L with screw holes in the arms. Angle irons are placed in 90-degree joints and screwed to the joints through the holes. They also come in many sizes.

Wire

Different types of wire are used in several of the projects in this book. Most are available at building supply dealers in rolls of different lengths, but you can sometimes get shorter pieces cut. You can trim and cut wire with tin snips or wire cutters, but always wear leather gloves when doing so. These types include:

→ Hog wire, also called woven wire, which is available in 3-, 4-, 5-, and 6-foot-high rolls. These rolls are quite heavy and awkward to handle, especially in the longer widths.

→ Poultry wire is available in a wide range of widths and roll lengths. It is a lightweight mesh wire that is primarily used for poultry fencing or as a trellis filler for plants to climb on.

→ Hardware cloth is a welded, galvanized wire with a square mesh, approximately ½ or ⅜ inch on a side. It's stronger than poultry wire but more expensive and is used for a variety of purposes. Quite often hardware cloth is installed in the bottom of cages for poultry and rabbits. I recommend hardware cloth here for the greenhouse benches.

Concrete

Concrete is used to embed poles for some of the projects in this book and for the floor in the attached greenhouse. Concrete is made by combining cement, sand, and crushed stone along with water in the proper proportions. A mix of 1 part cement, 2½ parts sand, and 3½ parts crushed stone is fairly standard. You can mix your own for small jobs with Portland cement (which is available in #80 bags), sand, and gravel. This is mixed to the proper proportions in a wheelbarrow or an electric-powered cement mixer. You can usually rent a mixer in most larger cities.

For larger pours like the attached greenhouse, however, you're better off purchasing ready-mix concrete delivered in a truck to the site. It's extremely hard to mix enough concrete in small batches for larger projects without having the material set up before you complete the pour. For more information on working with concrete you might be interested in reading *How to Build Small Barns & Outbuildings* by Monte Burch from Storey/Garden Way Publishing.

ESTIMATING CONCRETE

When you order concrete by the truck, it is measured in yards. A yard is 27 cubic feet or a volume measuring 3x3x3 feet. When figuring the amount of concrete needed to fill any square or rectangular area, the following formula can be used if all the measurements are in feet:

$$\text{Cubic feet} = \frac{\text{width} \times \text{length} \times \text{thickness}}{27}$$

For example, the concrete needed to pour a slab 9 × 18 feet and 4 inches thick would be:

$$\text{Cubic yards} = \frac{9 \times 18 \times \frac{1}{3}}{27} = \frac{9 \times 18}{27 \times 3} = \frac{6}{3} = 2 \text{ cubic yards}$$

Tools and Techniques

WITH THE RIGHT TOOLS you can do anything. With the wrong tools even the simplest jobs can be tough. Remember that sometimes the wrong tool isn't simply cheaply made or badly designed — sometimes the wrong tool is simply inappropriate to the task at hand. Fortunately, you don't need a shop full of expensive tools to construct the projects in this book. Most of them can be constructed with hand tools, although a few power tools can make the process easier and faster. If you don't already own the tools you need, I suggest you start with a few quality hand tools and perhaps an economical but good-quality power tool or two. Learn the basics with the hand tools so that the more complicated chores with power tools will come more readily. Of course, some expensive specialized tools can make particular jobs a great deal simpler.

Hand Tools

The basic hand-tool kit should contain a hammer, handsaw, tape measure, carpenter's square, combination square, hand brace and

bit, push drill and bits, 4-foot level, string line, chalkline, and carpenter's pencil. Purchase only good-quality, name-brand tools. With care, they'll last a lifetime and more. I have tools I inherited from my father, including some he inherited from his uncle. I imagine my children

With the correct tools almost anything can be constructed. Most of the projects in this book can be made with just a few simple tools.

A handsaw can be used for most outdoor project cutting chores. If you plan to do any ripping, you'll need both a crosscut and a ripping saw.

Handsaws

Handsaws come in two basic varieties: crosscut saws and rip saws. Crosscut saws are made for cutting across the grain of the wood while ripping saws are designed for ripping, which is cutting with the grain. A crosscut saw can be used for both chores, but it won't rip as easily as a ripping saw. Handsaws are also available with different numbers of teeth per inch (tpi). The fewer the teeth per inch, the faster and rougher the saw will cut. For most rough-cut exterior work and especially for use

will have them eventually. Good tools require less effort and, more importantly, are safer to use. Sharp tools are also much safer and more efficient than dull ones. Although I don't have space here to go into sharpening, there are many excellent guides on the subject. It is important to remember that a tool designed for a specific job is probably the best tool for that job. I discuss below several tools and jigs or aids you can build yourself to make some work easier.

If you're a beginning woodworker, you may be wondering how to learn how to make things. Most of the techniques required to build these garden and gardening projects are fairly simple. It is important, however, to take your time and fully understand each step or technique. For instance, careless measurements or a poor job of cutting can make it difficult to assemble a project without frustrating trimming and fitting. Use a carpenter's square to mark every cut to assure that each one will be square with the board's edge.

CUTTING WITH HAND TOOLS

Cuts made with handsaws will often be rougher than when using power tools. After making each cut, hold your square against the side of the board and the cut edge to determine the squareness of the cut. Then hold the square across the edge to make sure the cut is not slanted one way or the other. If the cut is not square, you can often remedy it by sanding with a block of wood and sandpaper. Or you may have to recut the piece. The old carpenter's saying, "I've cut the piece four times and it's still too short," is not entirely a joke!

When a project requires several pieces with the same dimensions, it's a good idea to cut all the pieces at the same time. But don't saw all the pieces for a project before you begin; you'll often find small discrepancies between your actual measurements and the plans, so it's usually better to measure as you go along by comparing the plans and the pieces already cut to assure the pieces fit snugly and properly.

Sand the edges of the project pieces before joining them together and you'll remove any splintering. This is even a good idea on "rough" outdoor projects as it also helps cut down on painful splinters.

with pressure-treated wood, 6 to 8 tpi saws such as the Stanley Short-Cut or Craftsman FastCut are excellent. If you're doing more finished work, you'll want a saw that has more teeth to the inch such as the Craftsman 12 tpi SmoothCut saw.

A good hacksaw is necessary when cutting metal sheets or pipe. Durable hacksaws are widely available at hardware stores.

Squares

In order to assure a project will fit together correctly, you'll need a few types of squares. The oldest and most basic type is the carpenter's square. These are available in either aluminum or steel. They are large — measuring 16 by 24 inches — and are L-shaped. Carpenter's squares are particularly useful with larger projects.

The combination square is much smaller. Its 12-inch blade has a central groove that allows a triangular body to slide along the length of the blade. Combination squares are most useful for marking boards to be cut, especially ones that are too small for a carpenter's square to be practical. The body is held against the edge of the stock and the blade used as a marking

A combination square is necessary for a wide variety of marking chores.

A carpenter's square is used to assure that projects are constructed squarely.

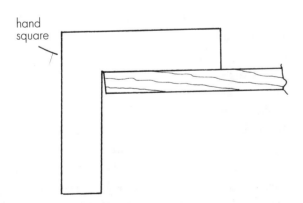

hand square

Whether you are an experienced or a beginning carpenter, the most important things to remember are to take your time, make your measurements exact, and always use a carpenter's square while you work to assure that your projects are being built square.

Bevel squares have an adjustable blade that can be set to different angles for marking cuts.

When using a handsaw, check the cut along its length and depth with a square to make sure your cut was at a full right angle.

A tape measure is good for most measuring chores. A locking blade allows you to position the tape to make multiple marks.

guide. To mark a line for ripping a board, the blade is loosened and the body is slid in or out to the ripping measurement needed. Then run the body along the edge of the board, holding a pencil at the end of the blade to mark the ripping cut line. Since there is also a 45-degree angle on the body, the square can be used to mark 45-degree cuts.

A T-bevel square is necessary for determining and marking angles such as those used on the around-the-tree bench. They most commonly have a steel head with a wooden arm. Because they can be adjusted to any angle, T-bevel squares can be used with protractors to set exact angles or match existing ones. It is laid on the stock with the wooden arm on the edge of the stock with the metal edge over the stock to be marked.

All of these squares are readily and inexpensively available. In general, steel versions are heavier and may rust, but they don't get bent as easily as aluminum or plastic ones.

Measuring Tools

I mentioned in one of my recent books that the fluorescent green tape measures from Stanley were so bright that I knew I had finally found a tape measure that I couldn't lose. Well, I've been looking for it for the past month, proving anything can get lost in my shop! In general, you'll want a 12-foot tape to carry on your belt for in-shop use and small projects, and a larger 25-foot tape for the bigger tasks in this book. A 100-foot tape ruler can be handy for laying out extensive fencing, although the 25 footer can be used in most instances. Regardless, make sure you get a tape measure with a locking blade since they're more handy.

Hammers

A 16-ounce curved-claw hammer is an all-purpose workhorse you can use on most projects, but a variety of hammer sizes and shapes can make some kinds of work much easier. Hammers are available with wood, fiberglass, and steel handles and in several claw styles. Just make sure you purchase a good-quality tool. Hammers are also very personal. I have a number of 12-ounce claw hammers I've accumulated over the years, some of which I inherited and some of which I picked up at auctions and farm sales. I often find myself picking up one particular hammer for a job because the balance and fit seems to suit me better than any of the others just then. When shopping for a hammer it's a good idea to feel the heft of several different ones; you can even ask the salesperson to let you swing it solidly on a surface to feel how it responds.

When you're framing with stock 2 inches or more thick, building wooden fences, or

In many instances, particularly when building more complicated pieces, it's a good idea to measure and cut pieces as you build. I often cut pieces a little longer and then hold the stock against the project and mark for the final cut.

TOENAILING

Sometimes you will need to nail one piece, often a stud, between other pieces that have already been fastened. Toenailing is the best way to handle such situations. Basically, toenailing is driving a nail at an angle through one piece of stock into another.

Toenailing is one of the hardest things for a beginning carpenter to learn because it involves holding one piece of wood in place while starting a nail and driving it in at an angle. To toenail a stud, first start an 8d nail about 1½ inches from the bottom at approximately a 60-degree angle. Position the stud on the plate and gently but firmly drive the nail into the stud until the nail contacts the plate. If the stud moves, reposition it and then sink the nail fully into the stud and plate. Once the first toenail has been sunk, the others are much easier to nail since the stud is secured.

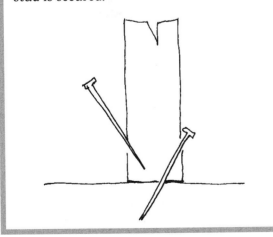

working on larger projects, a framing hammer is a better choice than a 16-ounce hammer. Framing hammers are available in 20- and 22-ounce weights. After a day of driving large 16d nails, you'll appreciate the heavier hammer's weight and balance. Framing hammers also have straight claws, which provide more leverage and make it easier to pull or remove nails.

The majority of the projects in this book are assembled with nails, and how you drive the nails reflects not only on the strength and longevity of the project but the appearance as well. If you don't often swing a hammer, get a block of wood and a handful of nails and spend a little time practicing. Using the proper hammer for the job is extremely important. Hitting the nail squarely on the head with a smooth, even swing is equally important. Don't try to drive the nail down with a few hard licks; use easygoing swings utilizing the weight of the hammer head to provide the force. Nails should be driven snugly into the wood but not so hard that you dent or damage the wood surface and break the wood into splinters.

USING A HAMMER

If you're not experienced using a hammer and nails, practice first on scrap stock. Learn to hit the nail squarely and to allow the weight of the hammer to drive the nail. Don't "choke up" too tightly on the hammer handle.

Fine work utilizes finish nails that are set below the surface of the wood. The nail holes are then filled with wood putty. Use a nail set is to drive the nail heads down below the wood surface.

USING A LEVEL

A 2-foot level can be used for most leveling work.

A 4-foot level makes leveling posts and other big jobs easier.

Choose the proper hammer for the job. Shown here is a framing hammer, which is useful for heavy-duty jobs.

Make sure to use enough nails to firmly hold the project together and check to make sure the nails don't protrude through the back side, which in the case of fencing and gates will often be a problem. When nails do protrude, hammer or bend the nails over, clinching them down flat against the wood surface.

Nail Set

If you're doing finish work on a project like a plant stand, you'll want to set the nails below the wood surface and fill in the gap with wood putty, a process that requires a nail set.

Levels

If you purchase only one level, a 24-inch level is the minimum size you should get. A 4-foot level is better for bigger jobs and can even be used on many smaller jobs. A level with a top-read window is occasionally handy. A string level can be used to lay out decorative fences and concrete slabs.

Wrenches and Pliers

A pair of adjustable wrenches and a variety of pliers are also needed for many chores, particularly fencing. If you plan to do any wire fencing, heavy-duty fencing pliers are a must.

Almost everyone needs a set of good-quality screwdrivers with a selection of both Phillips and straight blades.

Make sure to buy the best ones you can find since cheap imitations are less than worthless.

Screwdrivers

I can never get enough screwdrivers, mostly because I can never find the exact shape and size I need at a particular moment. Some companies sell complete screwdriver sets with a selection of Phillips and straight-blade sizes.

Clamps

A pair of large C-clamps and a pair of 4-foot bar or pipe clamps can hold projects together while you're fastening or gluing them in place.

You'll need a variety of pliers and wrenches. Heavy-duty fencing pliers are very important when working with wire fencing.

A variety of wood clamps are also helpful when assembling projects.

ENLARGING PATTERNS

Several projects in this book require enlarging squared drawings to make curves or cuts or to duplicate various patterns. Enlarging squared drawings is easy. Determine the size of the squares on the original. Count the squares in the original drawing and make up a copy with the same number of squares. Use a straightedge, ruler, and plastic drafting triangle to make sure the squares are actually square.

Number the lines on the squares, if you wish, on both the original and your full-sized squared drawing. Place dots on the original drawing where strategic lines of the pattern cross the squared lines. Count the lines on your enlarged pattern and place dots in the same corresponding positions. Then simply connect the dots, rounding any curves as needed to enlarge and complete the pattern.

A portable electric circular saw takes a great deal of the work out of cutting materials. A small and economical 6½-inch saw is quite sufficient for most chores.

Chisels

For many woodworking chores, chisels are indispensable. Chisels can be purchased in sets or individually. In general, I suggest purchasing a set. Normally chisels have beveled edges and you can choose from plastic and wooden handles. Plastic handles and wooden handles with a metal ring around the end can be hammered and will last longer than other types. Avoid cheap chisel sets. They can't be easily sharpened, won't hold an edge, and are simply dangerous.

Basic Portable Electric Tools

Although you can construct the majority of the projects with just hand tools, the proper power tools will make some work much easier and faster; in some cases, power tools are your only real choice. For instance, you'll need a router to cut the decorative post tops shown on page 72.

Portable Circular Saw

A portable circular saw is probably the single most important power tool you can own. It can crosscut, rip, or bevel any number of materials, including wood, composite materials, and metal with special blades. Portable circular saws are available in a wide variety of sizes ranging from a small 6½-inch blade up to giant 10-inch commercial versions, such as the Skil Dropfoot model. A 6½-inch blade cuts 2 inches at a 45-degree angle, which is all that's really necessary for these projects.

Choosing the correct saw blade to match the chore is also important with portable circular saws. Generally, I prefer carbide-tipped blades in spite of their added cost. If you're going to be cutting a lot of pressure-treated lumber you will need a saw blade designed specifically for that purpose such as the Irwin Marathon blade or the Skil Edge blade. A com-

Many of the projects in this book require stock to be ripped. One of the simplest methods is to use a portable circular saw and ripping guide.

A portable electric drill, especially a cordless model, is really handy when working where an extension cord would be a hassle or impossibility.

bination crosscut/rip blade is quite suitable in general, although you might wish to keep a more smooth-cutting blade for more "finished" projects.

Portable Drill

A portable electric drill is probably the second-most important power tool you can own. A drill can be used for many tasks besides simply boring holes and might even make them less "boring." Power drills are compared more by their bit size than by horsepower. Bit sizes range from ¼ inch up to ½ inch. A ⅜-inch portable electric drill in any of the major brand names is perfectly adequate for practically any garden project and will last a long, long time with reasonable care. When comparing horsepower, it's best to err on the side of power. You often get what you pay for.

Cordless models are an excellent choice because they can be taken almost anyplace without the hassle of providing electricity at the site, which can be an important factor in the garden or the back-forty. Good choices include the Stanley Cordless model and the Skil

Top-Gun, which comes with two rechargeable batteries so you can keep the drill in constant use. The Craftsman industrial-rated 8-cell drill/driver is also a very good heavy-duty model.

In most instances, folks purchase drill bits in sets. These can range from a large number of bits — often sold at discounted prices since the bits are soft carbon steel and will quickly dull with use — to the smaller sets of a half-dozen or so bits in a plastic case. These may or may not be good quality unless they are

---

COUNTERBORING

Counterboring is a technique to sink the head of a bolt or screw below the level of the surrounding wood, which is important, for example, when one piece of wood must cover another piece of wood where there is a bolt. First bore a hole large enough for the bolt and a wrench to tighten the bolt. Drill the hole to the depth of the bolt head. Then extend the hole with a smaller bit for the rest of the bolt.

brand name. Small sets contain commonly used sizes and a good way of getting the basic variety of bits needed for most garden projects. Just make sure the bits are a high-quality brand name or you're wasting your money. You can purchase some of the other more expensive specialty bits in the exact sizes you need for a specific project and add to your tool chest gradually. In addition to regular drill bits in sets, you might also consider buying a good set of blade or paddle bits for the larger boring chores. They're also more economical than "exotic" bits like forstners.

Specialty Power Tools and Accessories

Quite often expensive specialty tools have only a limited use. In some cases you may be able to rent or borrow the tools from friends. If you borrow, your friends can also show you how to use their tools.

Saber Saw

The scrollwork in the rose arbor's arch (see page 72) and other projects requires cutting

Additional portable power tools that can help with garden project construction include routers, sanders, and saber saws.

curved designs. A portable electric saber saw is an economical alternative to large stationary power tools. Most better saber saws average ¼ to ½ horsepower.

Router

A handheld router, such as the Sears plunge router, is necessary for routing a decorative groove in some of the fence posts. A good-quality router will generally be about 2 horsepower. A ¾-inch half-round router bit is required for the task.

Sanders

Some projects like furniture need sanding, which can be done most cheaply by hand with a block of wood and different grades of sandpaper. You can also speed up the job greatly with the use of a power sander. A belt sander is used for rough work. Finish pad sanders, such as the Sears Craftsman industrial finishing sander are good for smoothing up for a final finish. Quality belt sanders are usually about 1¼ horsepower.

Dowelling Jigs

A dowelling jig is used to join together pieces such as those that make up the arched top on the rose arbor. It is quite simple to operate and assures a strong and accurate joint. To begin the dowelling, the pieces to be joined are positioned together and a pencil mark is made across the joint for each dowel. The stock is then turned up and the pencil line extended across the faces of the joining pieces. The jig is set to position the drill bit half the width of the stock, placed in position, and clamped securely in place on the end of the stock. A drill bit in a portable electric drill is then used to bore the holes in both pieces for the dowels as the jig guides the drill for accurate hole positions. Stanley makes a good dowelling jig.

Power Fastening Tools

When it comes to the big jobs, power fastening tools can really save time and labor and make a big job go more smoothly. In some cases, the projects may even last longer. Air-compressor-driven tools are an excellent choice. Remember that power fasteners are designed primarily for contractors and are quite expensive. Although they will do the job more quickly and easily, plain old hand tools will work just as well with some time and muscle.

One tool I like for big jobs like greenhouses and fences is the ITW Paslode Impulse cordless power nailer, which utilizes a rechargeable battery and gas-charged cylinders instead of an air compressor. On fencing jobs, I tack-nail the boards on the posts with one nail to position the posts and then go back and finish-nail all the boards to the posts, usually in less than ten minutes. On several other projects I used similar tactics — tacking pieces in position and then using the power nailer to finish the job. The nailer can also use nails designed specifically for use in materials treated with CCA.

The Quick-Drive automatic screwdriver fastening system utilizes a coil of screws fed automatically to a portable electric drill. It's extremely fast and efficient for fastening screws.

Stationary Power Tools

The use of stationary power tools speeds up the process of cutting and shaping wood even more. Unfortunately, they're more costly and require a workshop and more skills than their equivalent hand or portable power tools. A table or radial arm saw would be a good first choice if you could only afford (or only have space for) one stationary power tool. It can be used for ripping, crosscutting, and — with the proper accessories — a number of other cutting and shaping chores.

A band saw is extremely handy for cutting curved pieces such as the arches for the rose

The Quick-Drive screwdriver system works well for heavy-duty fastening jobs.

If you have big jobs to complete, power fastening tools such as the ITW Impulse automatic nailer can cut down on the work time and make these chores easier. They can also prevent bursitis and other conditions caused by overwork with a hammer. The nailer shown is portable and can be taken to jobs without electricity on-site.

If you have the money and space, stationary power tools such as a radial arm or table saw can speed up many cutting and shaping chores and even improve most people's cutting accuracy.

arbor. A drill press can be used for precise boring jobs and, with additional attachments, several other chores. One less well-known solution, if your space is limited, is to purchase a multipurpose tool such as the Shopsmith. With the correct accessories, such a tool can combine a table saw, sander, lathe, drill press, and many others in one compact unit.

Digging Tools

If you need to set poles or posts in the ground you will need some digging tools. For just a few holes, a hand-operated clam-shell-type post-hole digger is more than adequate. If you're going to be doing a lot of holes you may prefer a power digger, especially if you're creating a long fence. Power diggers can often be rented; perhaps you can trade something with a neighbor who has a tractor-powered auger. In any case, you'll also need a long-handled and flat-bladed spade shovel. A handmade wooden

Drill presses are one of the most versatile kinds of stationary power tools.

Most people have a shovel in their garden anyway, and you will need it for the many projects that require digging holes for posts.

A post-hole digger is necessary for successfully handling larger, deeper holes.

A power auger makes fast work of digging lots of holes for a fencing project. These can usually be rented.

tamper helps when installing posts that need a tamped soil base.

Hand Tamper

When setting posts in earth, clay, or gravel, a hand tamper is a must for getting a post anchored solidly. You can make one quite easily from a 5-foot-long 2×4. Using a band saw or saber saw, cut 1 inch off both sides to create a 1½-inch by 1½-inch handle. Wood rasps, sandpaper, or a drawknife can smooth and round the handle portion.

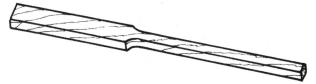

A homemade fence tamper can be used to tamp soil and gravel solidly around fence posts.

Fencing Tools

If you plan on having woven wire fencing, you'll need a fence clamp, which is merely two 2×4s clamped on either side of the wire as shown in the illustration. For stretching woven or barbed wire, you'll need a fence stretcher, although come-alongs can generally be substituted. Steel posts require a driver, which can be purchased inexpensively or you can weld your own as shown in the illustration.

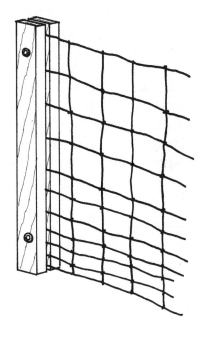

A handmade fencing clamp is useful for stretching woven wire.

Masonry Tools

If you intend to mix concrete to place around posts, a wheelbarrow, an old hoe, and a shovel are the basic tools required. A large trowel can be used to smooth down the concrete. For a concrete floor, an old garden rake can move the material around and a bull float, such as one from the Goldblatt Company, is excellent for finishing gardening project floors. Many of these tools can also be rented from tool rental companies.

Tool Safety

Both beginning and experienced woodworkers need to think carefully about how to be safe. Safety is extremely important anytime you're using hand or power tools. Handsaws, drill bits, and portable electric and stationary power tool blades, bits, and cutters are all sharp. They can do a great deal of damage even when they are standing still. Always keep a first-aid kit with antiseptic and wound wraps in your shop or close at hand. When cutting edges are moving, they're extremely dangerous. After almost forty years of carpentry, my father got just a little careless one day and stuck his finger in an electric jointer, which shortened one of his fingers. Used improperly, even a simple tool such as a hammer can be mighty dangerous, not to mention frustrating. Finger mashing occurs occasionally even with the best of us; pay attention to your work and know when you're too tired to be effective and productive. Unfortunately, I find that once you smack a fin-

ger you'll probably smack it again! You might as well get a pair of tweezers. Sooner or later you're going to get a splinter.

Use hammers only for their job. Carpentry hammers are not made for striking other metal objects such as chisels, bolt heads, and screwdrivers. Chips can fly off the head of a hammer and easily injure you or someone else. Use the proper tools for a chore.

Anytime you're working with sharp cutting tools or when you're hammering, you need eye protection. When using portable electric cutting or boring tools, safety goggles for eye protection and ear protection are also necessary. When sanding or cutting treated wood, wear a sanding or dust mask. Steel-toed boots are good to have when you drop heavy posts on your feet. When working with any power tools, wear comfortable clothes but avoid loose, floppy clothing that can be caught in tools and cause an injury.

Most of today's double-insulated power tools are safe to operate in ordinary outdoor situations, but common sense should prevail. Don't run them in a rainstorm or in an extremely wet situation. You may not get a shock from the tools, but you could get one from the extension cord connection. If at all possible, use a ground-fault interrupter when you plug them in.

My thoughts on safety are not intended to turn you away from carpentry generally or from using power tools. Used properly, according to the manufacturer's directions for safe operation and with all guards in place, tools are wondrous items. With attention to details and safety, carpentry is a safe and pleasant hobby and trade.

Sawhorse

Construction

Begin construction by laying out the compound angles on the top piece for the angled legs. You'll need a T-bevel square and combination square for this chore. Use a handsaw to make the initial cuts, then a sharp chisel to remove the material between the cuts to create the angled mortises for the legs.

Lay out the compound angles for the top and bottom ends of the legs and cut with a handsaw. Fasten the legs to the top with flathead wood screws countersunk below the surface. Make sure the sawhorse sits square. Measure and cut the leg braces and fasten them in place.

Sawhorse Materials List

1 Top: 2 × 6 × 36"
4 Legs: 1 × 6 × 23½"
4 braces: 1 × 6 × 13"

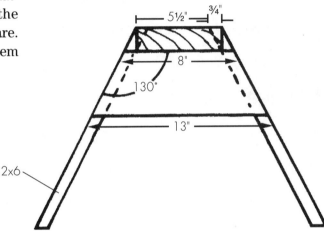

END ELEVATION

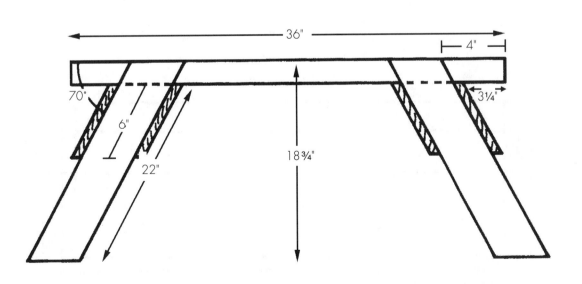

SIDE ELEVATION

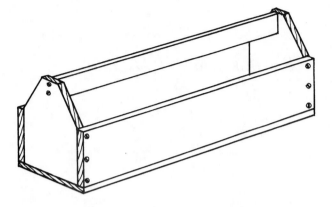

TOOLBOX

A toolbox provides a means of carrying and storing your tools, which is convenient with the outdoor projects in this book. You can purchase a toolbox or make up a simple wooden box such as shown in the drawing. Note that the box pictured is made entirely of 1x stock.

This simple, homemade toolbox can be used to carry and store many of your tools.

TOOLBOX MATERIALS LIST

1 Bottom: 1 × 8 × 31"
2 Ends: 1 × 6½ × 10"
2 Sides: 1 × 5½ × 31"
1 Handle: 1 × 2 × 29½"

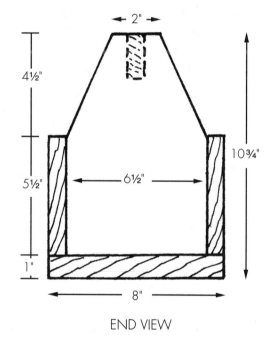

END VIEW

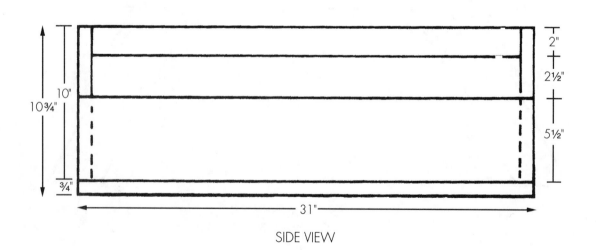

SIDE VIEW

WORKBENCH

Many of the projects in this book are best assembled in a workshop, which makes a sturdy workbench with a smooth top invaluable. A workbench can be purchased or you can easily make up your own with these plans. The workbench shown is made of 2x6s to provide a stout and efficient work surface for making whatever projects you tackle.

Construction

The first step is to lay out and cut the legs and rails to the correct length. Bore holes in the legs for the 8-inch lag screws (see illustration

WORKBENCH MATERIALS LIST

4 Legs: 2 × 4 × 34½"
4 End rails: 2 × 6 × 23"
2 Front and back upper rails:
   2 × 6 × 63"
1 Lower rail: 2 × 6 × 70"
6 Top boards: 2 × 6 × 72"
1 Top: ¼" hardboard × 30 × 72"
1 Backboard: ¾ × 8 × 72"
1 Tool board: ¾ × 3 × 72"
2 Tool board side braces: ¾ × 3 × 6"

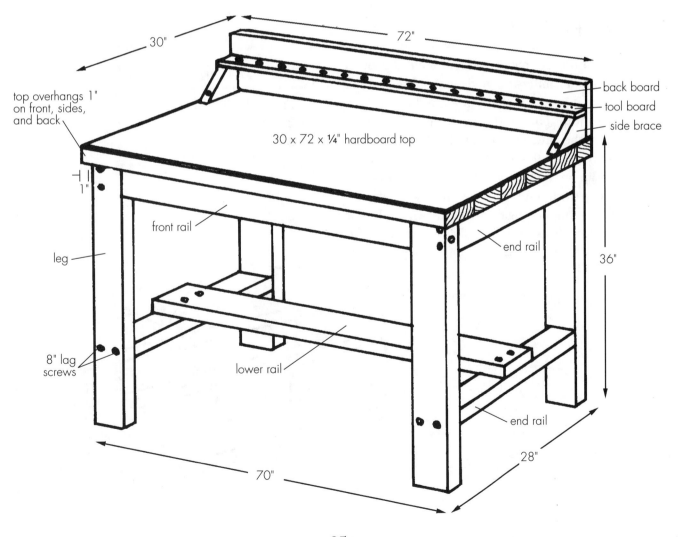

top overhangs 1" on front, sides, and back

back board
tool board
side brace

30 x 72 x ¼" hardboard top

front rail

end rail

leg

1"
1"

36"

8" lag screws

lower rail

end rail

70"

28"

SCHAUMBURG TWP. DISTRICT LIBRARY

for placement). Arrange two end rails behind the leg as shown and screw the lag screws through the leg into the ends of the rails. Make sure the assembly is square with a carpenter's square before tightening the screws. Attach the other leg and then construct the opposite end frame in the same manner.

Next, fasten the front and back rails to the end frames by bolting lag screws through the leg sides into the ends of the rails. Position the bottom support rail on top of the bottom end rails and fasten them together with lag screws.

Cut the top boards to length and rip the last one to the proper width. Fasten them on top of the frame with 16d common nails. Make sure the frame is square before the boards are securely fastened. Cover the top with a piece of ¼-inch hardboard to provide a smooth work surface. Once you've cut this to its proper size, install it with panel adhesive.

Rip the backboard to the proper width and cut to length. Then rip the tool-holding board, bore the holes to fit your tools, and cut the side braces to size. Fasten the tool-support board down on the top edges of the side braces using 8d finish nails. Then attach the tool-rack assembly to the backboard with 8d finish nails driven from the back of the backboard. Finally, anchor the tool-board assembly to the back of the top of the workbench with screws. Paint or stain and finish to suit.

MITER BOX

A miter box is a handy gadget for cutting joints and making miters (angled cuts) on small stock with a backsaw, which is a handsaw with a rigid metal bar on the back of the blade to stiffen the saw. The slots in the box guide the saw to make 90- and 45-degree cuts. The ½-inch lip on the bottom of the front allows you to keep the miter box still without clamping by pushing the box against the side of a table or workbench as you saw. Use a protractor to accurately lay out the 45- and 90-degree cuts.

MITER BOX MATERIALS LIST

1 Front: 1 x 3 x 12"
1 Back: 1 x 2¾ x 12"
1 Bottom: 1 x 4 x 12"

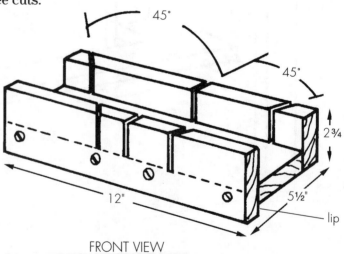

FRONT VIEW

Compass

A large shop compass is an unusual but help-ful tool you can construct yourself. It makes the chore of laying out large circles or arcs, such as those used to make the rose arbor and rose trellises, simple and straightforward. Use ½-inch stock cut to shape as shown.

Compass Materials List

2 Legs: ½ x 3 x 24"
1 16d nail
1 Lead pencil
Bolt, washers, and wing nut

Construction

Make a cardboard pattern the size and shape illustrated. Cut the wooden leg pieces to shape using a saber or band saw. Drive a 16d nail in the end of one leg and grind or saw the head of the nail off to create a sharp point. Bore a hole in the opposite leg so a wooden pencil will fit snugly in the hole. Push the pencil in place. Then bore holes through the center of the upper ends and fasten the pieces together with a bolt, washers, and a wing nut.

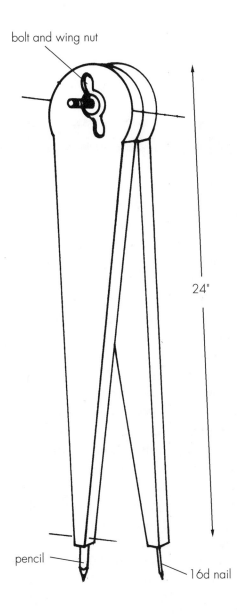

bolt and wing nut

24"

pencil

16d nail

Projects for the Porch, Patio, Deck, & Indoors

PLANTERS AND CONTAINER GARDENING

CONTAINER GARDENING has many advantages over simple row planting. Containers can be used in any garden but are especially effective for gardening in small spaces. One benefit is that you can place plants exactly where you want them and rearrange them as desired. Plants can be moved in or out of the shade or moved to suit a specific decor. Containers can be used to grow almost anything — depending on the size of the container, of course. Even dwarf fruit trees can be grown in containers in some parts of the country. Almost any type of plant you can imagine has probably been grown in containers ranging from discarded bathtubs to halves of wooden whiskey barrels. The most popular containers, however, are clay and plastic pots and wooden planters.

The latter can be purchased, but you can easily make your own and size the containers to your specific needs. You can also shape the boxes however you would like: square, rectangular, triangular, simple, elaborate, elongated, short, or tall. You can even build a trellis into a box for growing vining plants. Box containers can be placed on a deck, patio, or balcony; fastened to a window sill; or hung from porches and sunshades.

One design restriction for all containers is to have drainage holes to prevent plants from drowning. If you plan to place the boxes on a deck, however, you may wish to create a shallow holding pan to catch excess water and prevent it from leaching out of the box and staining the deck.

Regardless of the design, wooden plant containers must be constructed of insect- and rot-resistant materials. Redwood and western cedar are two popular choices. Another extremely popular material these days — often more available in some areas — is pressure-treated wood. Regardless of the choice of materials, galvanized fasteners must be used to prevent rust stains.

Although pressure-treated wood, cedar, and redwood do not need a finish, a protective coating designed for the material can add life to your container and spark up the appearance as well. You may even wish to paint or stain it.

PLANTER #1

Made of both treated plywood and treated 1×6s, this planter is designed to be big enough to hold plenty of soil and to keep flowers fresh and blooming all summer, even on the south-facing deck of our home in southern Missouri. It is essentially a plywood box with decorative trim strips added. Plans for square and rectangular versions are shown. I let mine weather to match our deck, but they could be finished other ways if desired.

PLANTER #1 (SQUARE) MATERIALS LIST

- 2 Sides: ⅜ plywood × 8 × 18"
- 2 Ends: ⅜ plywood × 8 × 17¼"
- 1 Bottom: ⅜ plywood × 18 × 18"
- 36 Vertical strips: ¾ × ¾ × 8"
- 4 Bottom trim strips:
  ¾ × 2½ × cut to fit 19¾"
- 4 Top trim strips:
  ¾ × 1¼ × cut to fit 19¾"

PLANTER #1 (RECTANGULAR) MATERIALS LIST

- 2 Sides: ⅜ plywood × 8 × 36"
- 2 Ends: ⅜ plywood × 8 × 11¼"
- 1 Bottom: ⅜ plywood × 12 × 36"
- 46 Verticals: ¾ × ¾ × 8⅜"
- 2 Bottom side trim strips:
  ¾ × 2½ × cut to fit 38"
- 2 Bottom end trim strips:
  ¾ × 2½ × cut to fit 13½"
- 2 Top side trim strips:
  ¾ × 2 × cut to fit 15"
- 2 Top end trim strips:
  ¾ × 2 × cut to fit 39"

Construction

Begin by cutting the sides and ends to size using a portable circular saw or a table or radial arm saw. Nail the four pieces together with 4d galvanized nails, enclosing the end pieces within the sides. Be very careful not to allow nails to split out and protrude inside or outside. If you happen to drive a nail too close to the edge and it does protrude, simply use a nail set to drive it back, remove it, and drive another in the proper place. Cut the bottom to the cor-

rect size and nail it down over the assembly, again making sure no nails protrude.

Rip the decorative vertical strips to the correct width, crosscut them to the correct size, and fasten the strips to the sides of the box you just created. I used 4d galvanized nails that I clinched (bent) over on the inside, but a better method would be to use #8 1-inch wood screws screwed in from the interior to anchor these pieces.

Cut the bottom trim pieces to width using a ripping fence in a portable electric saw or on

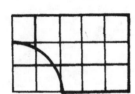

PATTERN FOR PLANTER FOOT
1 square = 1"

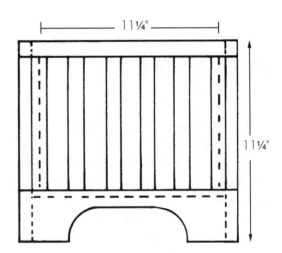

END ELEVATION, RECTANGULAR PLANTER

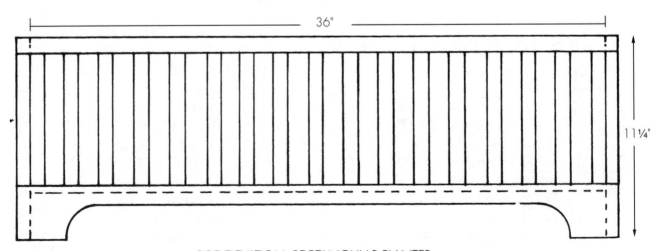

SIDE ELEVATION, RECTANGULAR PLANTER

64 Yard & Garden Projects You Can Build Yourself

a table or radial arm saw. Enlarge the squared drawing (as explained on page 16) and create a pattern for the feet. Transfer this to the stock and use a saber or band saw to cut the feet to shape.

Cut the mitered corners using a handsaw and miter box, a radial arm or table saw, or a portable circular saw set to 45 degrees. Fasten one piece of trim to the planter by driving screws up through the trim bottom into the bottom ends of the vertical strips.

I like to cut one end of the next mitered piece and then position it to make sure I get an exact measurement on the opposite end before cutting. I then cut to fit and anchor it in the same manner as the first. Cut the two remaining trim pieces and attach them through this same process.

Turn the assembly right side up and cut the top trim strips. Cut their corners at a 45-degree miter and anchor them down to the top ends of the vertical strips. Note that the top trim strips extend over the top of the sides. Also note that the top trim on the square planter is

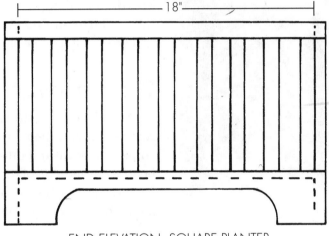

END ELEVATION, SQUARE PLANTER

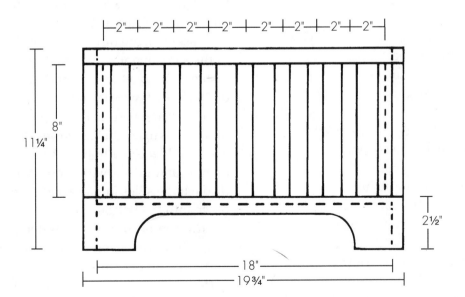

SIDE ELEVATION, SQUARE PLANTER

31

narrower than on the rectangular planter. After building the square planter, I decided the planter would be more balanced with a wider top trim. If you wish, you can simply change the width of the top trim pieces in the materials list.

Finally, bore six equal-spaced drainage holes in the bottom, with each hole ½ inch in diameter. You're now ready to finish the containers as you desire.

PLANTER #2 MATERIALS LIST

- 8   Sides: 1 × 6 × 18"
- 6   Ends: 1 × 6 × 18"
- 10 Vertical trim strips: ¾ × 1 × 17¼"
- 2   Bottom side cleats:
      ¾ × ¾ × 24", cut to size
- 2   Bottom end cleats, ¾ × ¾ × 15",
      cut to size
- 4   Bottom boards: 1 × 6 × 16½"
- 2   Upper side trim strips:
      ¾ × 1¾ × 25", cut to size
- 2   Upper end trim strips:
      ¾ × 1¾ × 21", cut to size
- 2   Bottom side trim strips:
      ¾ × 1 × 25", cut to size
- 2   Bottom end trim strips:
      ¾ × 1 × 21", cut to size
- 4   Feet: 1½ × 3½ × 3½"

PLANTER #2

This design is similar to Planter #1 except that this container utilizes solid 1×6 treated lumber and creates a deeper planter.

Construction

Start by cutting the side boards to the correct length and then cutting the vertical trim strips and the inside bottom cleats. Lay the four boards for one side of the planter together and fasten a cleat to the bottom interior with #8 1¼-inch wood screws through the cleat into the side pieces.

Rip the vertical side trim pieces to their correct width and fasten them over the side board joints with wood screws through the top and bottom cleats and the sides.

Assemble the other side and the two ends in the same manner. When all four are ready, fasten them together using 6d galvanized nails or #8 1½-inch wood screws.

Create the bottom by cutting the solid bottom boards to length to fit inside the box you've created. Place the bottom boards inside the planter and fasten with wood screws driven through the sides into the bottom boards, and down into the bottom cleats.

Rip the bottom and top decorative trim strips to their correct width and miter the corners. You can attach these to the planter with wood screws or galvanized nails driven through the upper and lower trim strips into the vertical trim strips on the outside of the box.

Cut the feet to the correct size and install them on the bottom with wood screws driven through the box bottom.

To finish, bore about six ½-inch drainage holes evenly spacedalong the bottom. You can now apply any paint, stain, or protective coating you wish.

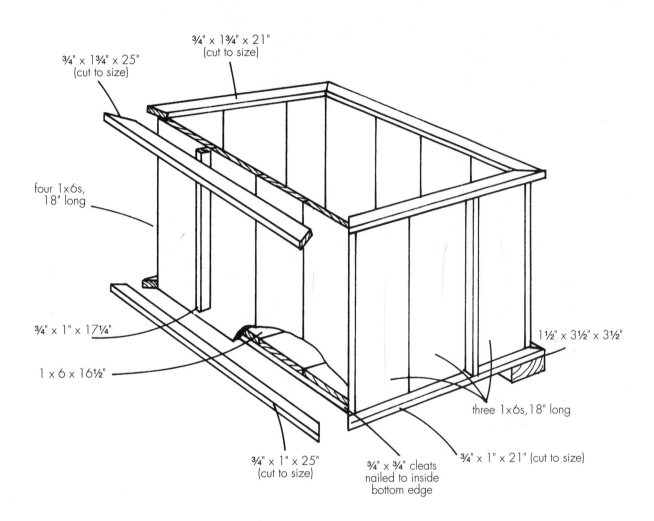

¾" x 1¾" x 21" (cut to size)

¾" x 1¾" x 25" (cut to size)

four 1x6s, 18" long

¾" x 1" x 17¼"

1 x 6 x 16½"

¾" x 1" x 25" (cut to size)

¾" x ¾" cleats nailed to inside bottom edge

¾" x 1" x 21" (cut to size)

three 1x6s, 18" long

1½" x 3½" x 3½"

WINDOW-BOX PLANTER

Window boxes are a great way of adding color to your home. Not only can they be enjoyed from outside the house, but they will bring sparkle indoors as well without the hassle and mess of actually growing plants inside. With some types of plants, you can attract birds — even hummingbirds — right to your window.

We constructed a window-box planter for our kitchen this spring and filled it with white petunias and red geraniums. To our delight it was steadily visited all season by a troop of the tiny birds, which was a continual pleasure while working in the kitchen.

Window boxes can be made in a wide variety of styles and types to suit your particular decor. They can also be made of a number of different materials. We constructed the box shown of rough-sawn western white cedar to match the trim and rough-sawn siding of our house. Although this design appears intricate and somewhat complicated to build, it is a relatively easy project.

Construction

You should initiate construction by ripping the stock to the needed width for the front, back, and ends before crosscutting these pieces to their correct lengths. Stand the two ends on edge on a smooth surface and fasten the back in place using 6d galvanized nails. Turn the unit over and fasten the front in the same manner.

Rip the bottom to the proper width, cut it to length, and fasten it down over the assembled

WINDOW-BOX PLANTER MATERIALS LIST

1 Front: ¾ × 4¾ × 58½"
1 Back: ¾ × 4¾ × 58½"
2 Ends: ¾ × 4¾ × 6¼"
1 Bottom: ¾ × 7¾ × 58½"
1 Front top trim strip: ¾ × 1½ × 60", cut to fit
2 End top trim strips: ¾ × 1½ × 9", cut to fit
1 Back top trim strip: ¾ × ¾ × 60", cut to fit
2 End support brackets: ¾ × 8 × 9"
1 Front apron: ¾ × 3 × 60"
2 End support cleats: ¾ × 1½ × 6½"
1 Back support cleat: ¾ × 1½ × 58½"

frame with 6d galvanized nails. Make sure to check and ensure the assembly is square with a carpenter's square before final assembly.

Prepare all the top trim strips by first ripping them to their proper width and then cutting to proper length. Miter the strips at their corners for a good fit around the planter top. Mitered cuts can easily be done with a fine-toothed handsaw and miter box. Fasten the top trim strips in place with 4d galvanized nails.

The next step is to cut the decorative end support brackets. Make a pattern using the squared drawing shown. Enlarge the pattern to 1-inch squares and transfer the pattern twice (side by side) to the stock by cutting out a cardboard pattern or using typing paper carbons beneath a paper pattern (see page 16).

The decorative scrollwork can be cut using a coping saw, portable electric saber saw, or band saw. Cut to the shape shown and sand all edges smooth.

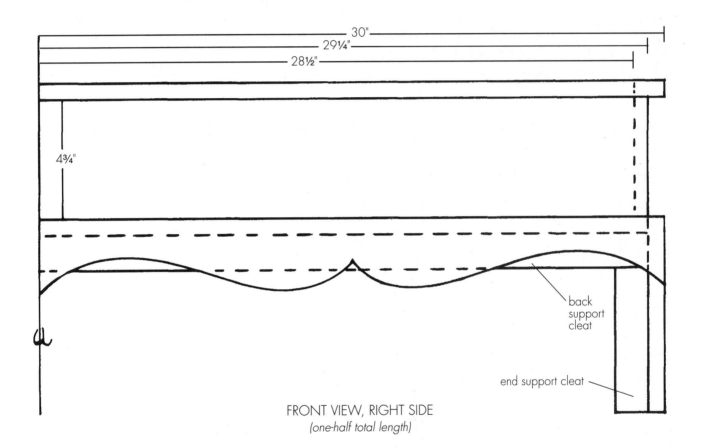

FRONT VIEW, RIGHT SIDE
(one-half total length)

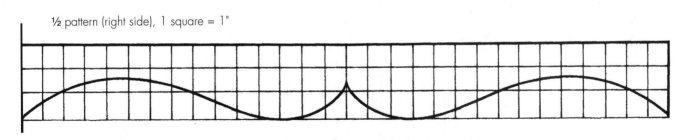

½ pattern (right side), 1 square = 1"

PATTERN FOR FRONT DECORATIVE APRON

With both ends cut, rip the back and end support cleats to their correct width and cut to length. Fasten the back cleat between the two end cleats with 6d galvanized nails driven through the ends. Square the back cleat against the back of the window box and fasten it with 8d galvanized nails through the bottom edge of the cleat and into the planter bottom. Nail the end cleats to the end support brackets with 6d galvanized nails through the supports into the cleats.

Enlarge the squared drawing for the front decorative apron and make a pattern by repeating it twice. Cut the stock to shape in the same manner as the end support brackets. Fasten the apron to the front edges of the ends with 6d galvanized nails. Drive 8d galvanized nails through the edge of shallowly cut areas on the apron into the planter bottom.

The window box pictured was given a coat of paint to match our house trim. To anchor the window box to the house, position it in place, level it with a 4-foot level, and drive nails or lag screws through the cleats into the house siding. Use lag screws in the back upper edge of the box, passing into the house siding at stud locations to provide further support. When filled with soil, window boxes can be quite heavy, so make sure yours is well anchored to the house.

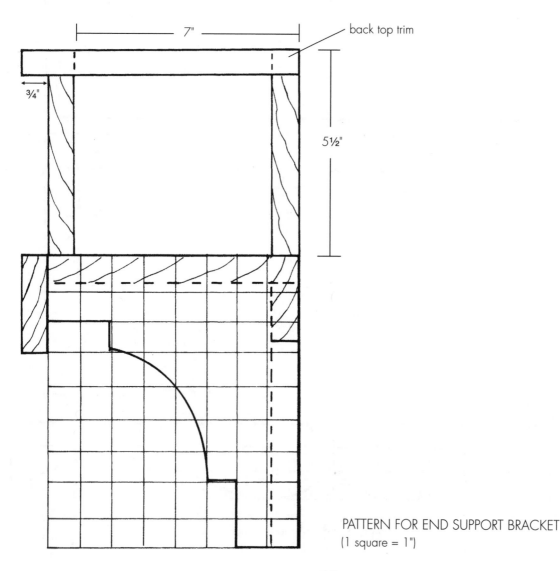

PATTERN FOR END SUPPORT BRACKET
(1 square = 1")

Window-Shelf Planter

Another even simpler planter to create is a shelf that holds potted plants outside beneath a window. You can arrange decorative pots on the shelf and change them as the seasons progress. This window-shelf planter is quite easy and makes a good Saturday project.

Construction

You can either rip the shelf board to the correct width or — in most cases — you can purchase precut stock of this width at many building supply dealers. Note the shelf is set ¼" below the front apron and end pieces to prevent pots from sliding or being accidentally pushed off the shelf board. If you prefer a more finished look, use finish nails and set them below the wood surface with a nail set.

Cut the decorative end pieces to the correct size and shape by enlarging and following the squared drawing. Fasten these in place by driving 6d galvanized nails down through the shelf board into the upper edges of the end pieces.

Cut the back and end cleats to the proper width and lengths and fasten them to the underside of the shelf

Window-Shelf Planter Materials List

1 Shelf: ¾ × 8 × 58½"
2 End pieces: ¾ × 8 × 9"
1 Front apron: ¾ × 3 × 60"
2 End cleats: ¾ × 1½ × 8¼"
1 Back cleat: ¾ × 1¾ × 58½"

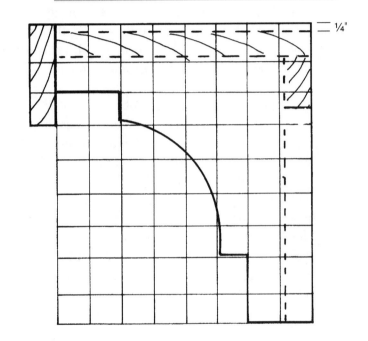

PATTERN FOR DECORATIVE END PIECES
(1 square = 1")

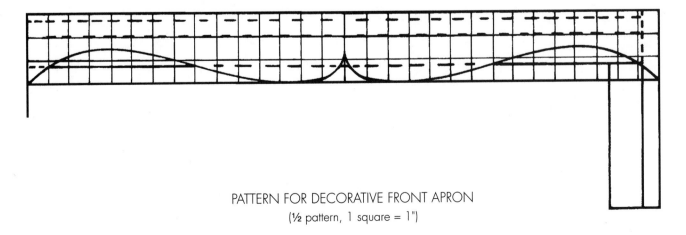

PATTERN FOR DECORATIVE FRONT APRON
(½ pattern, 1 square = 1")

board and to the end pieces with 6d galvanized nails.

Enlarge the squared drawing for the front decorative apron to its correct shape and size, making a mirror image to form a complete pattern, and cut. Attach the apron to the front edge of the shelf using 6d galvanized nails.

Anchor the shelf to your house below the window with lag screws driven through cleats. Level it both horizontally and vertically to make certain that it does not drain back toward the house.

PLANTING WITH WINDOW BOXES AND PLANTERS

Your new planters will need soil, which should be carefully prepared to suit the individual plant or plants that will inhabit the containers. Some plants, for instance, require an acidic soil. As a general rule, container soil should be fairly light and able to hold moisture and nutrients. The soil should also drain well. You can use either purchased commercial soil mixes or you can make up your own with 1 part garden soil, 1 part compost or humus, and 1 part sand. Vermiculite can be substituted for the sand to provide a lighter soil that will drain well but still hold moisture.

To plant, first place a layer of pebbles or gravel in the bottom to aid in drainage. Some experts also like to add a few pieces of charcoal in the bottom to act as a moisture "filter" to cut down on odors that might occur if the soil becomes too damp and/or moldy. Then fill the boxes to within a ½ inch or so of the top with soil. Add the plants.

All container-grown plants must be kept well supplied with the proper nutrients as per the plants' needs. Liquid fertilizers such as fish emulsion, Miracle-Gro, or homemade manure tea (made by submerging a bag of manure in a barrel of water) should be applied once a week. In addition to nutrients, the container-grown plants must be kept well watered and, during the heat of the summer months, that often means at least once a day.

PORCH AND PATIO PLANT STANDS

ONE GREAT ADVANTAGE of potted plants is that you can rearrange them as often as you want. Plant stands in particular can make displaying plants more attractive and rearrangement easy. Plant stands also add to the decor of a patio, deck, or porch. In the winter months the plant stands can even hold plants up off the floor in a sunroom or family room if there is enough light. For interior use, plant stands should have liners to prevent moisture from running onto the floor. Liners can be purchased, or you can even make them from such things as recycled milk cartons and old dishes.

Plant stands can be as simple or complicated as you wish. They can be left unfinished to match decks, or you can sand, stain and varnish, or even paint them to match or contrast with your room or house decor. I have included several different designs.

PLATFORM PLANT STAND

The simple stand shown is the easiest to make and actually makes use of a cut-off piece of a 4x4 fence post left from a fencing job. All wood scraps go in a huge heap by my shop. When I walk by the pile I often think of a project I can make with these scrap pieces. Using wood scraps is especially important with pressure-treated lumber, as it shouldn't be burned in a fireplace or stove because it can give off toxic fumes. As a result, I'm always looking for projects to use up end pieces and scraps of treated wood. I hate to throw any wood scraps away!

PLATFORM PLANT STAND MATERIALS LIST

- 1 Post: 4 × 4 × 24"
- 4 Legs: 2 × 4 × 12"
- 1 Top: ⅜ plywood × 12 × 12"
- 4 Top trim strips: ¾ × 1½ × 13½"

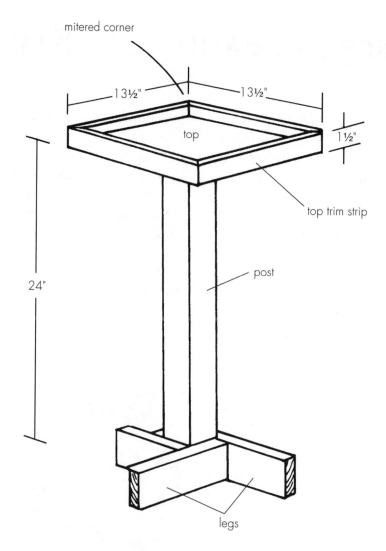

mitered corner

13½"   13½"

top

1½"

top trim strip

24"

post

legs

PLATFORM PLANT STAND

Construction

Since the cut-off fence post section was 24 inches long, I did nothing more than check the end with a square to ascertain that both ends were cut square. If you're cutting the upright from a full-sized post, first check the factory-cut end to make sure it is square. If it isn't, make a square cut there first. To ensure your cut is square, use a combination square to mark one side and continue around the post until all four sides are square. Your lines should meet where you began. The cut can be made using a handsaw or portable circular saw. Unless you have a big 10-inch-blade circular saw, you'll

have to make two cuts with a regular circular saw. If you follow the lines on all sides, the cut or cuts will be square. Use a block of wood with sandpaper wrapped around it to smooth up any discrepancies.

Cut the four "legs" to length from a 2x4. Once again, I used scraps from other projects in this book for these pieces. Smooth up both end cuts on each piece with a block of wood and sandpaper.

Lay the upright post on a flat work surface and fasten the first leg in place using 8d galvanized nails. If you wish to make the stand more decorative, use hardwoods and fasten the pieces together with finish nails. The holes should then be filled, the surface sanded smooth, and the entire project given a stain and finish coat.

Ensure the legs are attached to the post squarely or the stand won't sit level. To check squareness, lay a leg in position and place a carpenter's square on the post. One edge of the square should rest against the upper edge of the leg and the opposite arm of the square should align with the outer edge of the post. Move the leg in or out until it is square, then fasten in place securely.

For the next step, you'll have to extend the post and leg assembly out past the work surface edge. Start a couple of nails in the next leg piece, position it against the inside of the first and square with the upright post — again checking with a square — and fasten. Continue with the other two legs in the same fashion.

Cut the plywood top piece to size, which was a leftover piece from the garden cart. Make sure the top is cut squarely.

The top trim pieces are ripped from 1x materials, which can be marked on the stock at the width needed with a combination square set to the correct measurement and then cut with a hand ripping saw, a portable electric circular saw and ripping guide, or a radial arm or table saw.

The corners of the trim pieces are mitered. You can do this with a handsaw and a home-made miter box, or you can simply use a combination square to mark a 45-degree miter cut on the top edge of the stock. Then use the square on both the inside and outside faces to mark across the stock. Saw with a fine-toothed handsaw, following the lines on all three sides. Make the first miter cut, hold the stock against the plywood top, and mark for the next cut, which is made in the same manner. Start 8d nails in the mitered trim strip, stand the plywood piece on a smooth surface, and nail the strip in place. Make sure the nails are driven in at the approximate center of the plywood or they may come through on the other side.

Cut one end of the next mitered trim strip, hold it against the plywood edge and the two mitered cuts, and mark for the mitered cut on the opposite end. Nail this strip in position and continue until the other two trim pieces have also been installed. Turn the assembled top upside down and mark lines from diagonal to diagonal (corner to corner) to define the center. Then mark outward from the center 1¾ inches on each line. Use the combination square to mark the outline of the post top in this manner on the bottom of the top assembly, connecting each mark on the lines.

Place the top assembly down over the post assembly — checking that it lines up with the squared lines — and fasten with 8d galvanized nails.

MULTILEVEL PLANT STAND

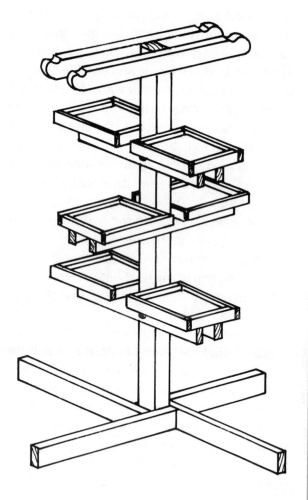

This tall plant stand can be used to fill in a corner of a deck or patio and can help you show off plants at different levels on the six paired shelves. The stand can hold a lot of plants! It's great for baskets and planters with overflowing and vining plants such as tuberous begonias, petunias, geraniums, ivy, and impatiens. In the winter months the stand can be used to hold bird feeders.

MULTILEVEL PLANT STAND MATERIALS LIST

  1 Post: 4 × 4 × 48"
  4 Feet: 2 × 4 × 16"
  6 Support arms: 2 × 4 × 16"
 12 Tray sides: ¾ × 3 × 12"
 12 Tray ends: ¾ × 3 × 10½"
  6 Tray bottoms: ¾ × 10½ × 10½"
  2 Hanging basket arms: 2 × 4 × 19"
  6 Bolts: ⅜ × 8" with nuts and washers

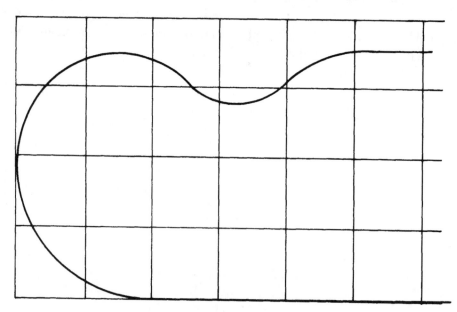

PATTERN FOR HANGING BASKET ARM
(1 square = 1")

Construction

Follow instructions for the post and foot assembly for the platform plant stand on page 40, adjusting height measurement to 48". Cut the support arms to length and mark attachment locations on post (see drawing). Fasten two arms at each point, on opposite sides of the post, with bolts driven through the support arms and into the upright post.

Make the plant trays in the same manner as the top tray for the platform plant stand. Plywood pieces are cut square and the side and end trim strips attached on the outer edges of the plywood. Fasten two plant trays to each set of support arms by nailing them down through their tops into the support arms with 6d nails.

Finally, cut the hanging basket arms. Make a pattern for the end notches (for hanging a basket or pot) from the squared drawing on page 42 and cut with a jig saw. Fasten the two arms to the top of the post with 3-inch lag screws, on opposite sides and at right angles to the first-level tray.

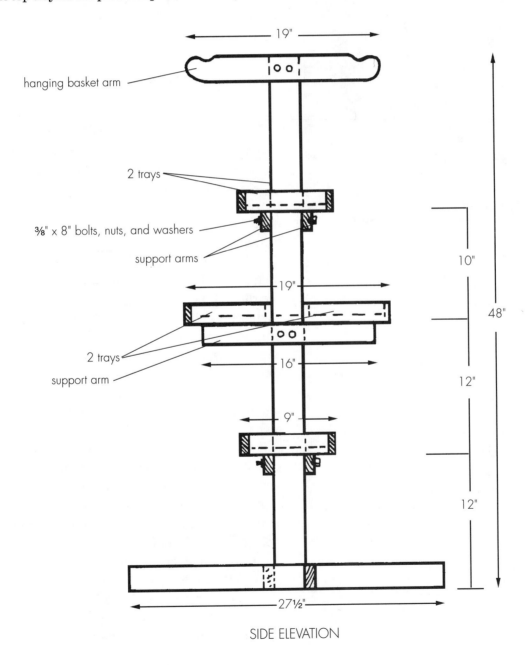

SIDE ELEVATION

PROJECTS FOR THE PORCH, PATIO, DECK & INDOORS

LATTICE PLANT STAND #1

After completing the outdoor screen and rose arbor projects (pages 72 and 146), my shop was adorned with several leftover pieces of wooden lattice screening, so I began looking for more projects to use up these pieces. The results are the next three plant stands.

This design is a good place to start. It's a plant stand and a decorative table for the patio, deck, porch, or sunroom. Although it seems somewhat complicated, this design is fairly easy to construct.

Construction

The entire basic framework is made of 2x2s. If the project is to be used outside, these should be of a good weather-resistant wood such as redwood or western white cedar.

If you can't purchase 2x2s, rip wider boards to width using a hand ripping saw, portable circular saw with a ripping guide, or a radial arm or table saw.

This is one of those projects where making multiple duplicate cuts saves time and effort — see the number of 16- and 13-inch pieces. Cut each size at the same time. It's extremely important that all cuts be square or the project will not assemble correctly. An "unsquare" square box is quite obvious. If you use a handsaw when cutting, mark with a combination square all around the stock and follow all lines with the saw.

Once all pieces have been cut to size, assemble the top frame on a smooth work surface by standing the two 13-inch top pieces on end, placing one of the 16-inch top pieces across them, and nailing down through the 16-inch pieces with 8d finish nails into the ends of the 13-inch pieces. Turn this assembly over and nail the other 16-inch piece in place in the same manner. Repeat for other square. Assemble the bottom section frame similarly. Use a combination square with its blade and body

LATTICE PLANT STAND #1
MATERIALS LIST

2 Top side pieces: 2 × 2 × 16"
2 Top side pieces: 2 × 2 × 13"
2 Bottom side pieces: 2 × 2 × 16"
2 Bottom side pieces: 2 × 2 × 13"
4 Legs: 2 × 2 × 13"
1 Top: ¾ × 18 × 18"
2 Lattice side panels: 11½ × 15½"
2 Lattice side panels: 12¾ × 15½"
8 Side trim strips: ¾ × ¾ × 13"

set like an L to check the frame for squareness at each stage.

Stand all four leg pieces on edge on the work surface and position the top frame on top of them. Drive 8d nails down through the top frame pieces into the upper ends of the legs. Once this construction is completed, turn the assembly upside down and fasten the bottom frame on the lower ends of the legs in the same manner.

Now for the latticework. Measure the inside of one side and cut the lattice to fit. It should fit snugly against the sides but be about ¼ inch short at the top and bottom to prevent any protrusion that could cause problems when installing the top of the unit. Fasten the latticework with brads through the latticework into the interior of the top and bottom frame pieces. Turn the unit completely over and cut and install the opposite side's latticework in the same manner.

Next, turn the unit over to one of the uncovered sides. Measure between the two installed lattice pieces and cut the latticework

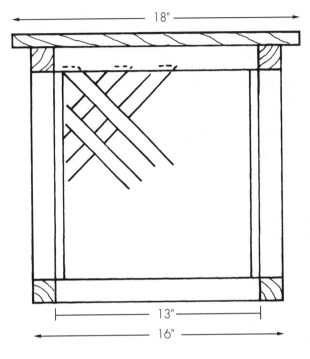

SIDE ELEVATION

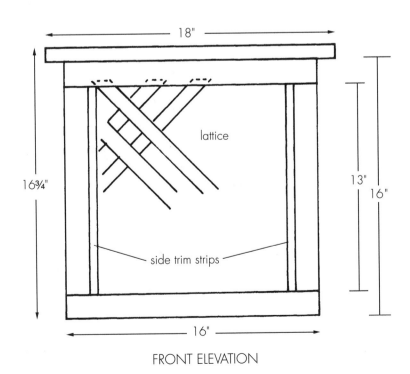

FRONT ELEVATION

Projects for the Porch, Patio, Deck & Indoors

to fit. Fasten this piece in place, then turn the unit completely over and cut and fit the opposite piece. With all lattice in place, cut the side trim strips for each leg and fasten them to the legs with brads to cover the unfinished lattice-work edges.

Stand the unit upright on a smooth surface. I made the top for my plant stand out of two pieces of ¾" scraps. But you can cut one whole piece if you have it. With two pieces, these can be joined together using a dowelling jig for a more finished look, but for most purposes — especially on a top this small — simply fastening them down on the upper framework will suffice. Cut each piece to length, ripping pieces to make up the width needed.

Fasten the top pieces on the top frame using 8d finish nails, setting the nails below the surface and filling the holes with wood putty. You can also use 8d galvanized nails.

This is also a great project to use up some scraps of treated plywood by edging the planter with trim as on the platform plant stand.

I think this project looks great painted. If you do paint it, you might wish to paint the lattice panels before installing them. As you will note from the photograph of this stand, the lattice shows through and needs to be painted inside and out. It's much easier to paint the panels first rather than trying to paint the inside of the stand.

LATTICE PLANT STAND #2

This plant stand matches the preceding project. Its height depends on your needs. We built this one to be level with our porch railing, but the stand could be taller or shorter. It again utilizes scraps of latticework.

Construction

Construction starts by ripping the legs and upper and lower frame pieces to a 1½-inch width from 2x4 stock, assuming you can't find 2x2 stock in your area.

Cut the legs and crosspieces to the correct length. Note that the center side rails are made of 2x4s. The center end rails are also 2x4s notched to fit around the end 2x4s.

With all framing pieces cut to the correct size, the first step is to stand an upper end rail and center end rail piece on a flat surface. Fasten a leg to the ends of these two pieces using either 8d galvanized nails or finish nails driven below the surface with a nail set. Once the two horizontal pieces are secure, fasten the bottom end rail to the leg in the same manner. Turn the assembly over and fasten the opposite leg down on the three horizontals. Assemble the second leg frame. Check at each step to ensure the assembly is square.

Stand the four upper and center side rails on end and position one end leg frame down over these and fasten. Turn the unit over and fasten the opposite leg frame in position in the same manner.

Measure the inside of one side and cut the lattice to fit, so that it fits snugly with about a ¼-inch clearance at the top and bottom. Fasten with brads through the latticework into the side. Turn the frame over and install lattice to fit. Measure the space left at each end between installed lattice pieces and cut end pieces to fit and attach. Cut the trim strips and nail them to the bottom and sides of each outside frame to conceal the cut edges of the latticework.

LATTICE PLANT STAND #2 MATERIALS LIST

4 Legs: 1½ × 1½ × 29¼"
2 Upper end rails: 1½ × 1½ × 10"
2 Bottom end rails: 1½ × 1½ × 10"
2 Center end rails: 2 × 4 × 10"
2 Upper side rails: 1½ × 1½ × 37"
2 Center side rails: 2 × 4 × 37"
1 Bottom shelf: ¾ × 8 × 40"
1 Planter shelf: ¾ × 9 × 36"
2 Bottom end trim strips:
   ¾ × ¾ × 10"
4 Vertical end trim strips:
   ¾ × ¾ × 5⅞"
2 Bottom side trim strips:
   ¾ × ¾ × 37"
4 Vertical side trim strips:
   ¾ × ¾ × 5⅞"
2 Side lattice pieces: 7¾ × 37"
2 End lattice pieces: 7¾ × 9"
2 Top end aprons: ¾ × 2½ × 15",
   cut to fit
2 Top side aprons: ¾ × 2½ × 42",
   cut to fit

Cut the top planter shelf piece to length and position it inside the frame resting on the protruding 2x4 edges. Fasten with 6d galvanized nails. Cut the bottom shelf piece and anchor it across the bottom horizontal end rails with 6d galvanized or finish nails that you then set and fill.

Attach the top end and side apron pieces flat along on the upper rail with 6d nails. Miter the corners for a good fit and finished look.

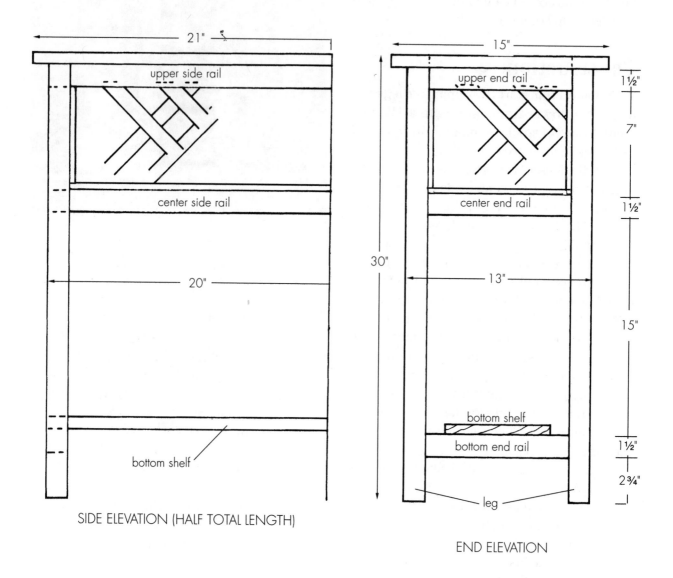

SIDE ELEVATION (HALF TOTAL LENGTH)

END ELEVATION

64 Yard & Garden Projects You Can Build Yourself

LATTICE FERN STAND

With its slightly Victorian styling, this lattice fern stand is designed to match the other two lattice plant stands (pages 44-48). It is constructed in much the same manner as the Lattice Plant Stand #1, except that the bottom horizontal braces are raised from the floor instead of being placed directly on the floor.

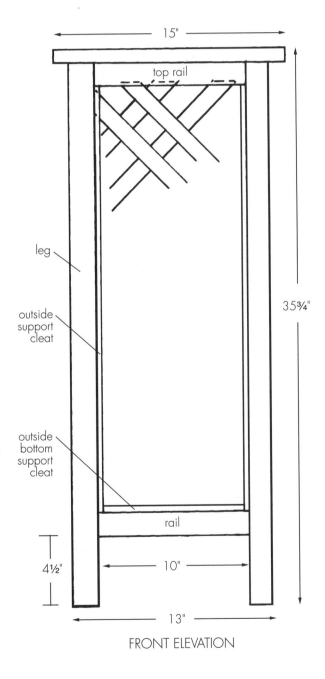

FRONT ELEVATION

LATTICE FERN STAND MATERIALS LIST

4 Legs: $1\frac{1}{2} \times 1\frac{1}{2} \times 35$"
8 Rails: $1\frac{1}{2} \times 1\frac{1}{2} \times 10$"
8 Outside support cleats: $\frac{3}{4} \times \frac{3}{4} \times 27\frac{1}{2}$"
4 Lattice panels: $9\frac{7}{8} \times 29$"
4 Outside bottom support cleats: $\frac{3}{4} \times \frac{3}{4} \times 8\frac{1}{2}$"
1 Top: $\frac{3}{4} \times 15 \times 15$"

Construction

Begin by placing two of the rails on end on a smooth work surface. Place one leg across the rails, adjusting rails to proper locations. Attach with 8d finish nails through the leg and each rail. Turn assembly over and attach opposite leg. Use a combination square with its blade and body set like an L to check for squareness at each stage.

Repeat leg assembly for opposite side. Join two sides with remaining rails. Attach lattice panels, as described for Lattice Plant Stand #1 on page 45. Add outside support cleats along vertical and bottom edges of latticework. Finish by attaching top using 8d finish nails, setting them below the top's surface and filling holes with wood putty.

GROW-LIGHT STANDS

IF YOU'VE EVER grown plants from seed or collected a large number of houseplants, you know how useful a grow-light stand can be. I've included two designs here: a basic multi-shelf structure mainly for seed starting; and a more finished indoor single-shelf unit that will fit in any room of the house.

BASIC GROW-LIGHT STAND

It seems I've always planted seeds — tomatoes, peppers, flowers — every spring. I've planted them in plastic trays, on windowsills, on top of the refrigerator, and just about any other flat space that either provided warmth or sunlight. I have also had a little trouble growing seeds with fairly specific needs such as bottom warmth and seeds that need more light than filters through a window on a winter day. Several years ago I tried hanging fluorescent lights over the top of a table in my basement. I was amazed at how easy it was to sprout and raise troublesome seeds. I start a large number of seeds to fill a vegetable garden that feeds our family of four, the flower bed, and those pots on our porch and deck. More than once I've found my office desk — which is close to a window — overflowing with plants about mid-March. But not anymore. Not since I decided to build this grow-light stand.

The unit had to be fairly large to hold so many plants, yet light enough to easily move it outside from our family room as the weather warmed. The stand actually consists of three wooden trays fastened to a 2×2 framework. You can readily equip the stand with a standard 4-foot fluorescent tube over each plant-holding tray. I've started a *lot* of plants very successfully with the stand.

GROW-LIGHT STAND MATERIALS LIST

3	Tray bottoms: ½ plywood × 24 × 60"
6	Tray sides: ¾ × 2½ × 58½"
6	Tray ends: ¾ × 2½ × 24"
4	End uprights: 2 × 2 × 63"
2	End cross pieces: 2 × 2 × 24"
1	Long top brace: 2 × 2 × 63"
14	Corner braces: 2 × 3" angle irons, or 2 × 3 × 3" wood blocks
3	Fluorescent light fixtures: 4'

Construction

Begin by constructing the trays, which are made of ½-inch-thick pressure-treated plywood for the bottom and a ¾-inch-thick band of treated wood around the edge. Rip the material for the tray sides and ends using a table saw or a portable electric circular saw fitted with a ripping guide. Once the pieces have been ripped to shape, lay them out on a flat surface such as a workbench or garage floor. Cut the bottom pieces from the plywood; make sure you cut them squarely and smoothly. Lightly sand all cut edges to remove any splinters. Attach the tray bottoms to the sides and ends by hammering the 4d galvanized nails through the bottom. Once the trays have been assembled, run a bead of bathtub caulk around the inside joint to completely waterproof the joints.

Cut the end upright pieces, which will have to be ripped from 2×4s with a table or radial arm saw or a portable circular saw and ripping

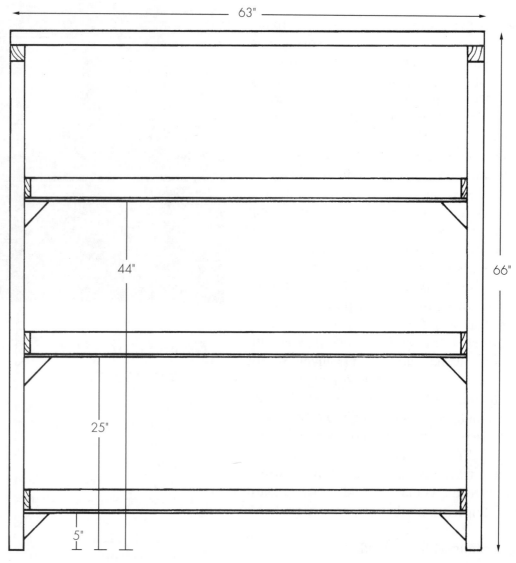

FRONT ELEVATION

guide. Cut the pieces to the correct length, then lay all four together on a flat surface. Measure for the position of the trays and mark across all 2×2s at the same time using a square.

Lay out two of the end upright pieces, stand a tray on end on top of them, and fasten the parts together with #10 1½-inch screws that pass through the tray end into the 2×2s. Stand a second tray in position and do the same thing. You may find that you need to brace the trays in place or have someone hold them until you get them solidly anchored. It's also a good idea to insert just one screw in each tray upright joint at this time. With all three trays anchored, place the opposite end upright on top of the trays, and make sure the trays are positioned and spaced properly. Again anchor with only one screw at each joint. Stand the entire assembly upright on a flat surface and use a square to make sure the assembly is square in all directions. Then further anchor the trays to the uprights with another screw in each joint.

The framework must be very rigid even though the trays give some support. Two methods can be used. The simplest is to use angle irons fastened to the bottom of each tray and the inside of the uprights. As often happens to rural folks, I didn't happen to have angle irons on hand the day I constructed the plant stand. Instead of driving to the hardware store, I used the second method: I substituted wooden blocks cut on a 45-degree angle from 2×6s for angle irons. Support and bracing are provided by #10 2-inch screws counterbored and driven through the corners of the blocks into the tray bottoms and uprights as well as screws inserted through the uprights into the blocks.

To stabilize the upper light hanger, I attached a 2×2 crosspiece across each pair of end uprights and then a second 2×2 long top brace connecting the tops of these cross pieces.

To hang the fluorescent light fixtures, screw eyes are fastened beneath the upper long brace and to the underside of the two higher trays. The lights I used are simply the widely available shop fixtures that come with a plug

on a short cord and two chains to suspend the lights. The chains can be used to raise or lower the lights to keep them the proper distance from your plants for the best growth.

The plant stand can be left as it is, or given a coat of protective oil coating (such as Thompson's Water Sealer), stained and varnished, or painted. One addition I might make is to add casters or rollers to the bottom feet so the stand can easily be rolled out onto the deck for warm, sunny spring days.

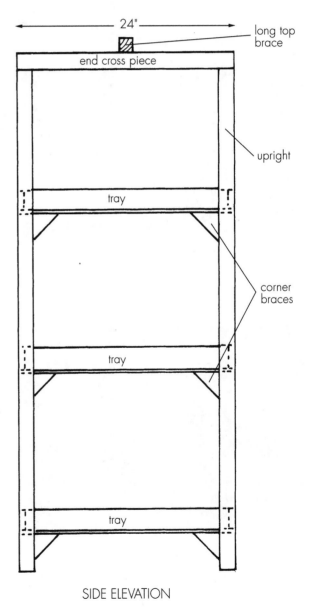

SIDE ELEVATION

The basic frame is assembled with galvanized nails.

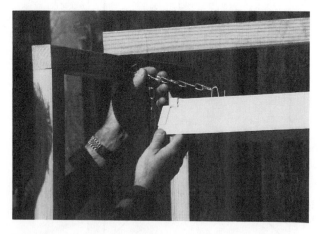

Eye hooks are screwed to the end crosspieces to support grow-light fixture on lightweight chains. The lights are raised or lowered by the chains.

My first season with the stand was a real success. I used a combination Moist-Rite tray with a soil heating cable from Harris Seeds to start petunias, impatiens, pansies, geraniums, and even some mums for the coming fall. The tray system worked quite well with almost 95 percent germination on petunias and 75 percent on impatiens. Bottom heat and fluorescent light provide an ideal seed-starting environment. I think next time to start a larger number of plants at the same time, I'll use a soil heating mat. Since the trays are somewhat small, I found I had to keep working at transplanting plants out of them so I could start more seeds.

INDOOR GROW-LIGHT STAND

If you wish to keep houseplants over the winter and/or to start flowers and vegetables from seed using a grow-light and heated seedbeds, this attractive stand can prove quite useful. The stand should be made of materials to match the decor and furniture of your home. Economical white pine, usually purchased as shelving material, or fancy hardwoods such as oak are good choices. This design differs greatly from the basic grow-light stand in appearance and size so it can be used indoors year round. We now use the large basic stand in the greenhouse and this small stand indoors in the family room to overwinter plants and to start seeds. This stand would be especially appreciated by an African violet grower.

The stand is designed to hold a single fluorescent shop light or grow-light fixture. An undercabinet fluorescent fixture might also be used. The stand can also be positioned next to a window for even more effectiveness. The design shown has the plant shelf at the height of our family-room window. You may wish to adjust the shelf height to fit the height of your window.

The unit shown is also constructed to hold two Harris Moist-Rite seed-starting trays with soil heating cables. A grow-light combined with a heating cable and bottom-watering tray prevents many of the problems associated with hard-to-grow seeds such as petunias, impatiens, pansies, and geraniums.

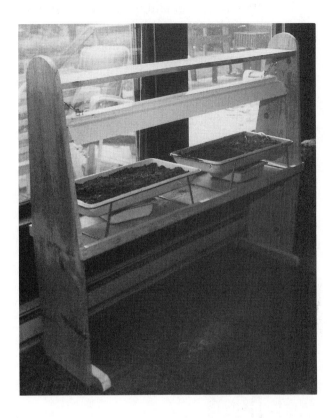

INDOOR GROW-LIGHT STAND MATERIALS LIST

- 2   End boards: ¾ × 11½ (1x12 shelving board) × 44"
- 2   Feet: 2 × 2 × 16"
- 1   Upper support piece: ¾ × 6½ × 53"
- 1   Shelf: ¾ × 11½ (1x12 shelving board) × 53"
- 2   Shelf trim pieces: ¾ × 1½ × 54½"
- 1   Fluorescent light fixture: 4'

Construction

Because this project was designed to actually be a "piece of furniture," more care is needed in its construction than for many of the rougher outdoor projects in this book. The needed techniques are quite simple and even a first-timer shouldn't find the project difficult.

You can also build it entirely with hand tools, although power tools will make the job much easier and faster.

Start by enlarging the squared drawing (page 57) and making a full-sized pattern for the upper portion of the boards. Cut the end boards to the proper length and transfer the pattern onto them. Before cutting, measure down from the top and, using a carpenter's square, mark a squared line across the board at the location for the upper support piece. If you don't do this now you'll find it hard to locate the square position once the board has been cut. You might as well mark the position lines for the bottom shelf as well.

The rounded upper ends can be cut using a portable electric saber or scroll saw. Then cut the straight lines between the rounded end and sides using a portable electric saw or handsaw. You can also quite easily make the entire cut in one pass with a band saw. Cut the rounded ends of the feet in the same manner. Once these have been cut to the proper size, sand all edges smooth with a piece of sandpaper held around a block of wood or with a power sander.

With the ends and feet shaped and sanded smooth, lay the end boards on a smooth surface and fasten the feet to their bottom edges using 6d finish nails. Set the nails below the surface of the wood about ⅛ inch using a nail set.

Cut the upper support piece and the shelf to the correct length and rip the support piece to the proper width. The latter can be done using a portable circular saw with a ripping guide or a handsaw. A ripping handsaw makes the chore easy. To lay out the width, slide a combination square set to the proper measurement while holding a pencil at the end. Use a block of wood and sandpaper or power sander to smooth up the ripped edge of the support piece.

Position the two end assemblies on edge on a flat surface and fasten one end of the

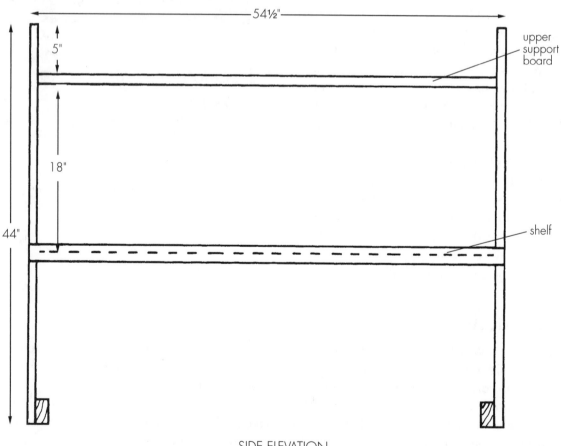

SIDE ELEVATION

64 Yard & Garden Projects You Can Build Yourself

shelf board to one end piece using 6d finish nails driven from the outside into the ends of the shelf. Fasten the opposite end assembly to the shelf board in the same manner. Then nail the upper support piece in place, making sure it follows the line drawn as a guide before the decorative upper ends were cut.

Rip the shelf trim pieces to width, crosscut them to their proper length, and sand their edges smooth. Then fasten them to the edges of the bottom shelf and to the end boards using 6d finish nails.

Set all nails below the wood surface using a nail set. Fill in the nail holes with wood putty or plastic wood. Sand the entire project smooth. Then stain, finish, or paint.

Finally, install small screw eyes in the lower side of the upper support piece. Hang the shop light or grow-light on these, adjusting the height of the light above your plants by raising and lowering the chain on the hooks. You can also install an undercabinet fluorescent fixture following the directions that come with the light, although these are not adjustable.

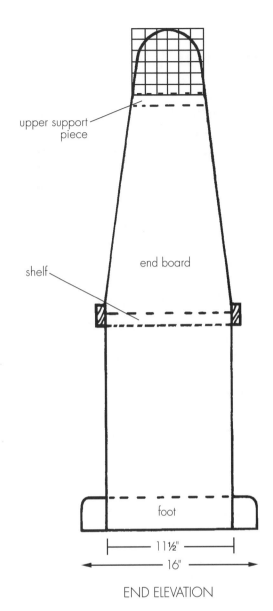

upper support piece

end board

shelf

foot

|— 11½" —|

|← 16" →|

END ELEVATION

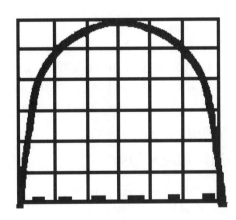

PATTERN FOR UPPER PORTION OF END BOARD
1 square = 1"

Projects for the Porch, Patio, Deck, & Indoors

PRODUCE SHELVING, BIN, AND TABLE

THROUGH MANY YEARS of raising a family and having lots of company for dinner, we've always grown a big garden and preserved enormous amounts of food. In fact, friends often laughed at my many gardens, even if they didn't hesitate a second at a dinner invitation! Our Ozark hilltop farm has few "flat" spots with any soil left, so we have three large gardens spaced around our farmstead on the only available areas. One garden includes almost a half-acre of corn, and we often put out one hundred pounds of seed potatoes. The results end up in hundreds of jars of vegetables, fruits, jams, jellies, sauces, pickles, and the like. An early step, of course, was to build storage shelves in our cellar for all the produce jars.

The potatoes, sweet potatoes, and apples from our orchard require storage as well. For many years we used boxes — wooden, cardboard, and even discarded shop racks — to store these crops. Nothing seemed to work quite right until I went to the shop and constructed a sturdy, open-framed bin to hold potatoes and other produce.

These projects are fairly simple and can be constructed of easily purchased, economical materials. The produce bin is designed to be made of precut wall studs, some of the cheapest 2×4s you can buy. Just make sure you select sturdy stock without knots or splits. The shelving is constructed of #4 shelving pine 1×12s and has a ¼-inch plywood back to provide support and to prevent jars from sliding out the back. The front trim lip keeps jars from sliding off the front and strengthens the shelves.

PRODUCE SHELVING

Do some picking if possible at the building supply yard to find shelving boards without loose knots or splits.

The shelving is made in sections so it isn't too bulky to carry or move. This design is also stronger than a single long shelving section.

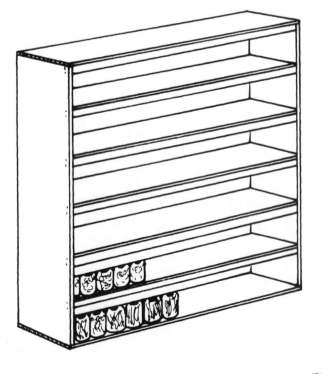

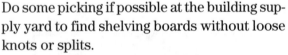
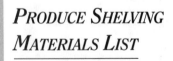

PRODUCE SHELVING
MATERIALS LIST

1	Back: ¼" plywood × 4' × 6'
2	End boards: ¾ × 11½ (1×12 shelving) × 70½"
5	Shelves: ¾ × 11½ (1×12 shelving) × 46½"
2	Top and bottom boards: ¾ × 11½ (1×12 shelving) × 48"
12	Shelf support cleats: ¾ × 1 × 10¾"
6	Front trim strips: ¾ × 2 × 46½"

Construction

Cut the two end boards to their proper length. Measure and mark the location for each shelf on both boards, which you can do easily by laying them together on a smooth surface. Then use a combination or carpenter's square to mark across the boards on their interior sides for the shelf locations. Measure ¾ inch down from each line and mark the locations for the top of the shelf support cleats.

Rip the shelf support cleats to the proper width using a handsaw, portable circular saw with a ripping guide, or radial arm or table saw.

Cut the cleats to the proper length and fasten them to the end boards along the cleat lines (¾ inch beneath the top of the shelf line). Use glue and 4d ring-shank nails.

Cut the top and bottom boards and all shelves to the proper length and sand their cut ends to remove any splinters caused by the cutting. Then position one end board on its edge on a flat work surface and fasten the bottom and top boards in place. Next fasten the shelves in place over the cleat board by nailing through the end into the ends of the shelves using 6d ring-shank nails. Make sure the shelf rests securely on the shelf cleat. Nail through the top

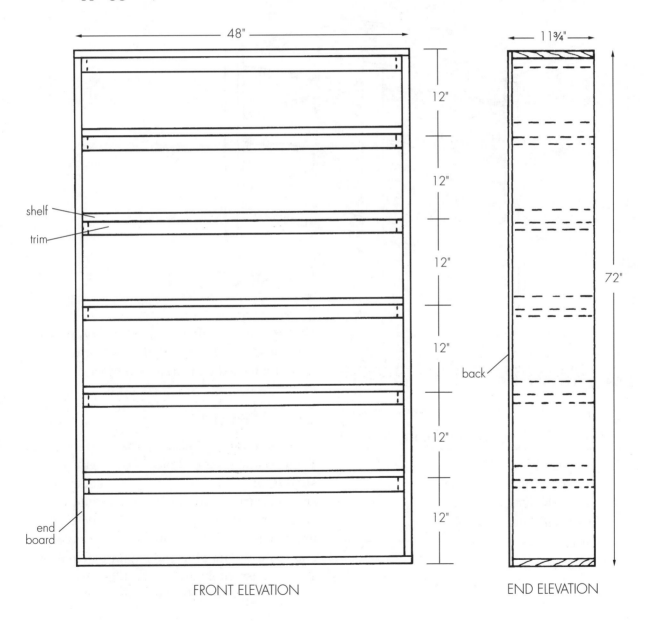

FRONT ELEVATION

END ELEVATION

of each shelf into the cleat in the same manner. Install the opposite end board similarly.

Turn the unit over on its front surface and measure. Trim the ¼-inch plywood back to size. Square up the assembly with a carpenter's square and install the back using 4d ring-shank nails. Then turn the assembly on its back and cut the front trim strips to size. Rip them using a hand ripping saw, portable circular saw with a ripping fence, or radial arm or table saw. Fasten in place beneath shelf boards (see drawing) with 8d finish nails to the front edge of the shelves, cleats, and the inside of end boards. Set the heads below the wood surface with a nail set and fill the nail holes with wood putty. Stain, finish, or paint to suit.

Incidentally, if your basement or cellar stays wet you may prefer to build the shelves of pressure-treated plywood or to set the shelving unit up off the floor on concrete blocks or bricks.

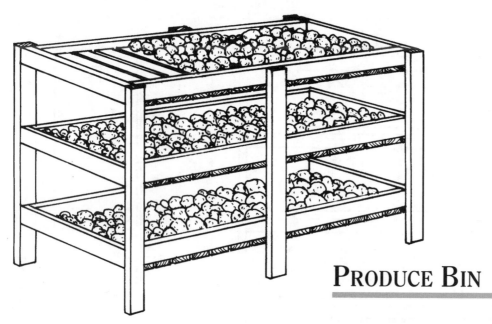

PRODUCE BIN

The produce bin is constructed entirely of 2×4s and is made by assembling three separate shelf racks that are then fastened to the legs.

Construction

First cut the shelf side pieces to length. Then cut the shelf end pieces to length. To assemble one shelf, lay two side pieces on a smooth surface and position one end piece across the edges of the two side pieces. Fasten in place with 16d nails driven through the end piece and into the ends of the side pieces. Turn the assembly around and fasten the opposite end piece in the same manner.

PRODUCE BIN MATERIALS LIST

6	Legs:	2 × 4 × 48"
6	Shelf ends:	2 × 4 × 24"
6	Shelf sides:	2 × 4 × 72"
51	Shelf slats:	2 × 4 × 24"

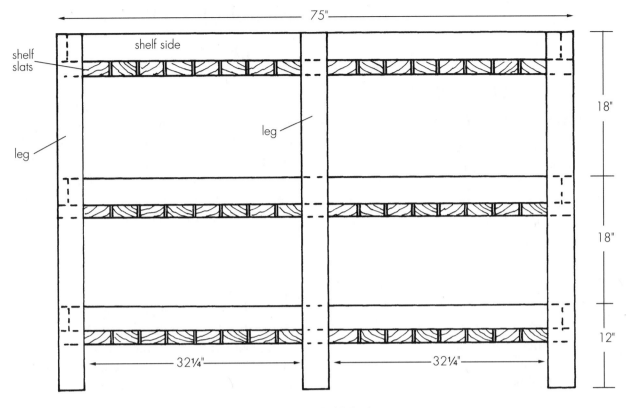

SIDE ELEVATION

With this assembly lying flat, use a carpen–ter's square to ensure it is square. Cut the shelf slats. Assemble 17 slats across the bottom of the frame, approximately ½ inch apart to allow for good airflow and to provide a dry storage rack. Nail slats to shelf sides with 16d nails. Assemble the remaining two shelf racks in the same manner.

With all three racks completely assembled, stand them on edge on a flat work surface at their approximate spacing from each other. Lay the three legs for one side across the racks and space racks and legs as shown in the drawing. Legs are square with corners of racks. Use a carpenter's square to ensure the assembly is square, then fasten the legs to the shelves us-ing 16d common nails. Turn the unit over and install the opposite three legs in the same man-ner. Again, make sure all are square with the assembly.

You may wish to paint or finish the rack for ease in cleaning.

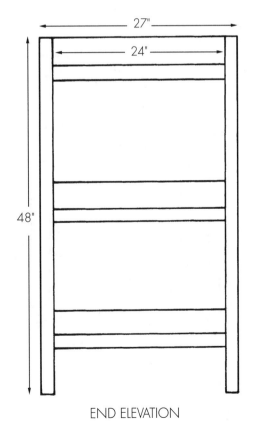

END ELEVATION

61

PRODUCE CLEANING TABLE

PRODUCE CLEANING TABLE
MATERIALS LIST

4   Legs: 2 × 4 × 35¼"
4   Side rails: 2 × 4 × 48"
4   End rails: 2 × 4 × 24"
Top: ¾ plywood × 35 × 56"
      or 7 top boards 1 × 6 × 56"
Dishpan or small sink

PLUMBING
4   Plastic water pipes
2   Els
1   Hose connector
1   Faucet bib connector
1   Faucet
2   Plumber's straps, 6"

Carrying vegetables — especially root crops such as radishes, turnips, onions, and beets — to the kitchen sink for cleaning often results in a messy and muddy kitchen. We've found over the years that tomatoes ripen better on a table under a shade tree outdoors, and picking the just-starting-to-turn-red tomatoes allows the plants to produce a lot more. So with the large amount of tomatoes we usually grow, we were looking for an outside table to wash and hold ripening tomatoes.

Our answer was simple: a sturdy, weather-proof table. The top of the table has a cutout for a plastic dishpan, which is our outside removable "sink." The water is supplied from a pipe and hose-bib faucet. The bottom end of

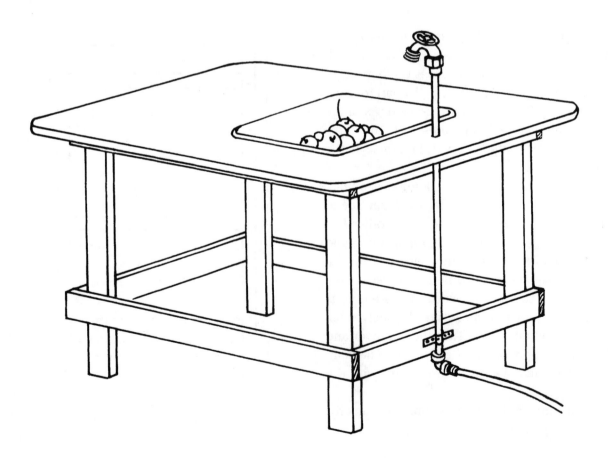

the pipe is fitted with a hose adapter so a garden hose can be hooked to the pipe to provide water. If you want, you could drop an actual small sink in place and add a faucet set to complete the water supply. With a sink you will have to adapt a hose to the drain as well.

In any case, the bottom framework of the table can be of pressure-treated wood or a weather-resistant wood such as redwood or western cedar. The top must be untreated plywood or redwood or western cedar rather than pressure-treated wood, as the latter is not acceptable for use on surfaces where it might come into contact with food.

Construction

The construction is fairly straightforward and simple. Begin with the leg and bottom framework. It's a good idea to first cut all the pieces to the correct shape.

Then lay two legs on a smooth work surface and fasten two end rails onto the legs at the appropriate places (see illustration) using 16d galvanized nails. Keep the ends of the rails flush with the edges of the legs. Make sure the assembly is square by checking with a carpenter's square before nailing the pieces solidly together. Assemble the opposite end leg frame in the same manner. Then stand the assembled end leg frames on edge and join them on one side with two side rails to one side, nailing with 16d galvanized nails and checking that the assembly is square. Turn the assembly over and attach the opposite two side rails.

If you are using solid wood for the top, cut the top piece to length and fasten. Note that the top piece should be as smooth as possible and free of knots or rough surfaces that can't be hosed off and cleaned easily. For this reason, heartwood redwood is a good choice for the surface. It is smooth and soft with little grain burring or raising when wet.

Fasten the top piece to the leg frame with 8d galvanized nails. Make sure these nail heads are driven down just slightly below the surface

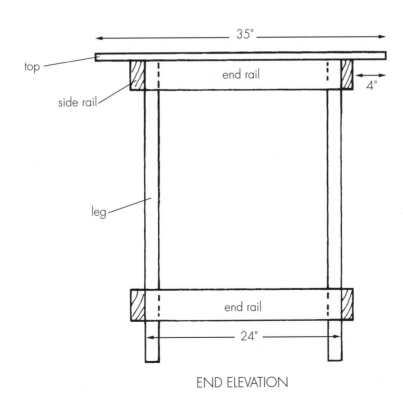

END ELEVATION

of the wood so you can wipe and hose the table off simply. Once the top piece is securely fastened, sand all edges smooth and round the corners with a router.

Place the sink or removable dishpan in position and mark the location. Bore four ⅜-inch holes — one at each corner of the sink's location — and then use a saber saw to cut out the opening by connecting the holes. Sand the edges of the opening smooth and drop in the dishpan or install the sink.

Assemble the water supply system with plastic tubing, an elbow, a nipple, and then a hose-bib faucet located over the sink or dishpan. Fasten a hose adapter on the bottom end of the plastic tubing so a hose can be attached. Use pipe or plumber's straps to anchor the plastic piping solidly against the back of the table.

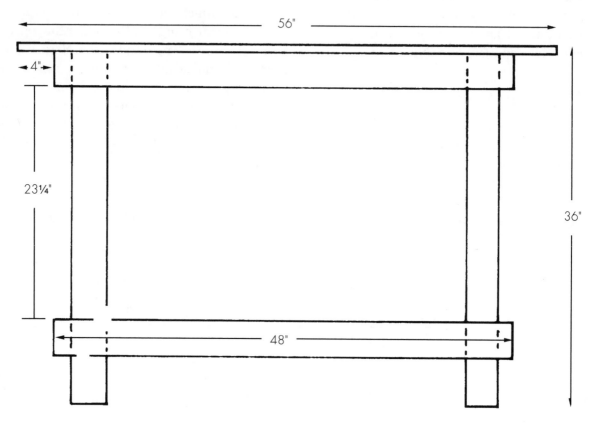

56"

4"

23¼"

36"

48"

SIDE ELEVATION

PATIO CHAIR
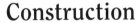

Deck and patio chairs are extremely popular items and fairly easy to make, although they take some attention to detail to cut the pieces precisely, as well as some special tools and techniques. The chair shown utilizes a dowelling jig to fasten the side frames together. A band saw or saber saw is needed to round the corners of the frame and, if you really want to add to the appearance, all edges of the frame can be rounded with a router.

Choosing the proper wood is also important. Treated wood can be used for the project but "softer," more attractive woods such as cypress, cedar, or perhaps redwood are better choices. Untreated woods are also more traditional for patio furniture.

Construction

Start by cutting all the pieces for the side frames to their correct sizes, ripping the narrow strips using a table saw, radial arm saw, or a portable circular saw with a rip fence. Cut the rounded ends of the horizontal pieces to shape using a band saw or saber saw. The side frame pieces are joined with dowels. Lay out the pieces for each side in position on a flat surface and mark the two dowel locations at each joint in the side frames. Use a dowelling jig to bore holes.

Assemble the frames by placing glue in all the holes, inserting dowels, and tapping the pieces together. Use bar clamps to squeeze the frames together. Make sure the frames are assembled square with a carpenter's square, then wipe away excess glue before it dries. Allow the frames to set overnight before sanding their surfaces smooth to remove any other excess

PATIO CHAIR MATERIALS LIST

4	Side frame horizontals: 1½ × 3½ × 24"
4	Side frame end verticals: 1½ × 3½ × 17"
6	Side frame center verticals: 1½ × 2 × 17"
2	Side seat supports: 1½ × 2 × 21"
2	Front and rear seat supports: 1½ × 2 × 21"
7	Seat boards: ¾ × 3 × 24"
2	Back side supports: 1½ × 2 × 30"
2	Back horizontal supports: 1½ × 2 × 21"
10	Back boards: ¾ × 3 × 24"
Brass wood screws:	
68	#8 1¼"
16	#8 2½"
6	Brass bolts and nuts: #12 3¾"

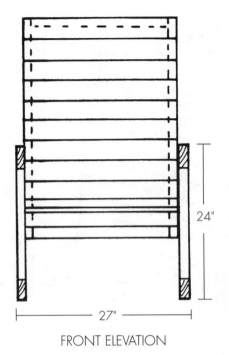

FRONT ELEVATION

24"

27"

back boards

back side support

brass bolts

side frame
horizontal

side frame end vertical

side frame center vertical

side seat support

32¾"

24"

7"

5"

10½"

7" 5" 5" 7"

24"

SIDE ELEVATION

glue. Now you can round off the edges with a router.

Next, cut the seat side supports to their correct length and width, then cut the seat boards to the correct length. Lay the two seat side supports on edge and place the ends of all the seat boards across them. Fasten the seat boards to the seat side supports with countersunk flathead #8 1¼-inch brass screws. Make sure the assembly is square. Cut the front and rear seat supports and fasten them between the seat side boards with countersunk flathead #8 2½-inch brass wood screws.

Assemble the back boards and supports in the same manner. Place back on top of rear back edge of the seat board, then fasten it with 3-inch wood screws driven up through the bottom of the rear seat support board.

Stand the seat assembly on its side on a smooth work surface. Mark the locations for the seat assembly on one side frame (see drawing), and position frame on the seat. Bore holes for #12 3¾-inch brass bolts and fasten. Turn the assembly over and position the opposite side frame. Locate, bore, and install the top bolt and nut. Stand the assembly upright on a flat surface to make sure it sits evenly, then bore and install the other two bolts. Apply a finish of your choice, stain, or paint if desired.

Chaise Lounge

This chaise lounge is made to match the style of the patio chair (page 65). It has a back support that props the back upright and, when dropped down, allows it to lay almost flat.

Construction

The construction is quite similar to that of the patio chair. Start by cutting all the pieces for the side frames to the correct sizes, ripping the narrow strips using a table saw, radial arm saw, or a portable circular saw with a rip fence. Cut the rounded ends of the upper and lower pieces to shape using a band saw or saber saw. Lay out the pieces in position on a flat surface and mark the dowel locations at each joint in the side frames; then use the dowelling jig to bore holes.

Assemble the frames by placing glue in all the holes, inserting the dowels, and tapping the pieces together. Use bar clamps to squeeze the frames together. Make sure the frames are square by checking with a carpenter's square, and wipe

Chaise Lounge Materials List

4	Side frame horizontals: 1½ × 3½ × 24"
4	Side frame end verticals: 1½ × 3½ × 14"
6	Side frame center verticals: 1½ × 2 × 17"
2	Side seat supports: 1½ × 2 × 60"
2	Front seat legs: 2 × 4 × 14½"
2	Front and rear seat supports: 1½ × 2 × 21"
16	Seat boards: ¾ × 3 × 24"
2	Back side supports: 1½ × 2 × 30"
1	Back horizontal support: 1½ × 2 × 21"
10	Back boards: ¾ × 3 × 24"
2	Back brace supports: ¾ × 1½ × 14"
1	Back brace dowel: 1 × 22½"

Brass wood screws:

104	#8 1¼"
20	#8 2½"
2	Brass bolts and nuts: #12 3¾"
2	Brass butt hinges: 3"

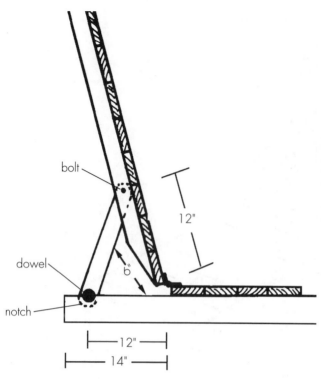

bolt

dowel

notch

12"

6"

12"

14"

DETAIL OF BACK BRACE ASSEMBLY, SIDE ELEVATION

away excess glue before it dries. Allow the frames to set overnight, then sand the surfaces smooth to remove any other excess glue. If you desire to round off edges with a router, do so at this time.

Cut the side seat supports to length as well as the front and rear seat supports. Cut a notch 2 inches from the end of each side seat support for the back brace dowel (see illustration). Fasten the front and rear seat supports between the side supports using countersunk #8 2½-inch brass flathead wood screws. Make sure this assembly is square. Then cut the seat boards to the proper length and fasten them in place on top of the seat frame using #8 1¼-inch wood screws. Cut the front seat legs to the proper length and attach them to the side seat supports with #8 2½-inch wood screws.

Position the seat assembly on its side on a smooth work surface, mark the locations of the

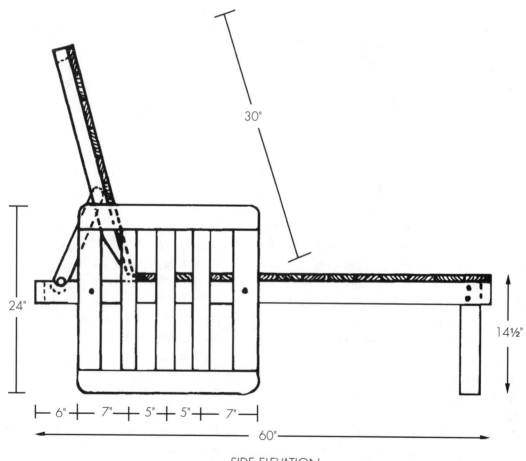

30"

24"

14½"

6" 7" 5" 5" 7"

60"

SIDE ELEVATION

64 Yard & Garden Projects You Can Build Yourself

seat assembly on one side frame, and position the side frame in place. Fasten using #8 2½-inch wood screws. Turn the assembly over and position the opposite side frame in place. Locate, bore, and install one screw. Stand the assembly upright on the flat surface to make sure it sits evenly, then bore and install the other screw.

Cut the back side supports to their proper lengths as well as the upper back support. Fasten the upper back support between the side supports using #8 2½-inch countersunk flathead wood screws. Cut the back boards to the proper length and width and install with #8 1¼-inch flathead countersunk wood screws. Make sure this assembly is square.

Cut the swinging back braces to length, round their ends, and bore the holes in their bottom ends for the support dowel. Cut the dowel to the proper length, place glue in the holes, and install the dowel. Lay this assembly out flat to assure the back braces are both in the same position on the dowel.

Once the glue has dried, install the back support assembly to the back assembly using #12 3¾-inch brass bolts and nuts. Countersink the bolt heads on the outside of the back assembly so it can swing down between the side frames.

Install the back assembly by first placing the support dowel in position in the notches cut in the side support pieces. Position the lower back in place on the edge of the back seat board and fasten with two 3-inch brass butt hinges. Finally, stain and finish or paint.

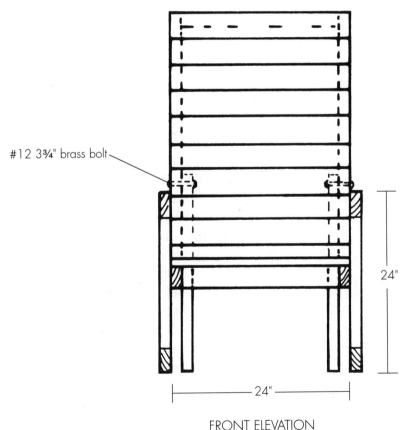

FRONT ELEVATION

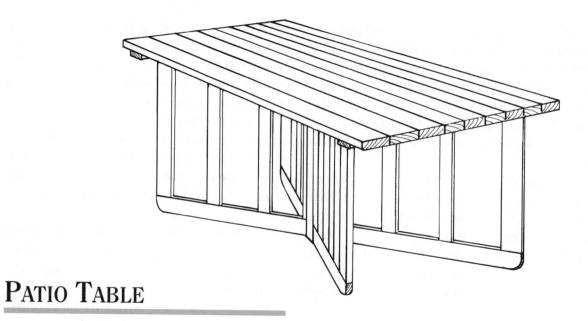

PATIO TABLE

Designed to match the patio chair and chaise lounge (pages 65–69), the table is constructed in basically the same manner. I suggest using the same type of woods and finish.

PATIO TABLE MATERIALS LIST

- 2 Main frame horizontals:
  1½ × 3½ × 54"
- 2 Main frame ends: 1½ × 3½ × 20"
- 7 Main frame center uprights:
  1½ × 2 × 20"
- 4 Side frame horizontals:
  1½ × 3½ × 26¼", cut to fit
- 2 Side frame outside ends:
  1½ × 3½ × 20"
- 2 Side frame inside ends:
  1½ × 1½ × 20"
- 6 Inside frame uprights: 1½ × 2 × 20"
- 2 Main frame cleats: 1½ × 2 × 27",
  ripped to fit
- 2 Main frame cleats: 1½ × 3 × 27",
  ripped to fit
- 2 Top cleats: 1½ × 3½ × 30"
- 10 Top boards: 1½ × 3 × 60"

Screws:
- 40 #12 2¼" round-head brass
- 24 #12 1½" flat-head brass

Construction

If you've constructed the patio chair and chaise lounge, you'll already have a good bit of practice in assembling the dowelled support frames. Start by cutting all the pieces for the support frames to the correct sizes before ripping the narrow strips using a table saw, radial arm saw, or a portable circular saw with a rip fence.

Note that the structure consists of one main frame with two side frames. The edges of the side frames abutting the main frame must be ripped at the angles shown before assembly (see drawing on page 71).

Cut the rounded ends of the upper and lower pieces to shape using a band or saber saw. Lay the pieces out in their position on a flat surface and mark the dowel locations. Use the dowelling jig to bore holes for the dowels at each joint in the side frames.

Assemble the frames by placing glue in all the holes, inserting the dowels, and tapping the pieces together. Use bar clamps to squeeze the frames together. Check with a carpenter's square to make sure the frames are assembled square. Wipe away any excess glue before it dries, allowing the frames to set overnight; then sand their surfaces smooth to remove any other excess glue. If you do want to round off the edges with a router, now is the time.

Rip the center frame cleats to the proper angles (note that there are two different sizes). Then stand the main frame upright on a smooth surface and prop it in place. Position a side frame in its proper position against the main frame and fasten solidly using #12 1½-inch flat-head countersunk wood screws. Position the opposite side frame and anchor in the same manner.

Rip the top boards to the correct width and cut to length. Cut the top cleat boards to proper length. Position the top boards upside down on a smooth surface, making sure they are square and that the ends meet properly. Then position the cleat boards on top of them and fasten with #12 2¼-inch round-head screws.

With the top upside down, place the support frame upside down on the top. Anchor with 1¾-inch by 1¾-inch support cleats on each side of the support frame, with #12 2¼-inch round-head wood screws through the cleats and into both the top and support frames. Stand the assembly upright and stain, finish, or paint to suit.

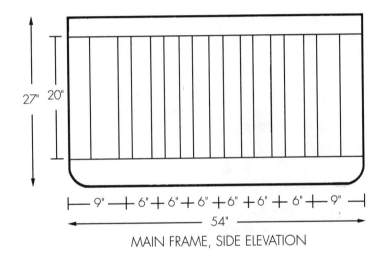

MAIN FRAME, SIDE ELEVATION

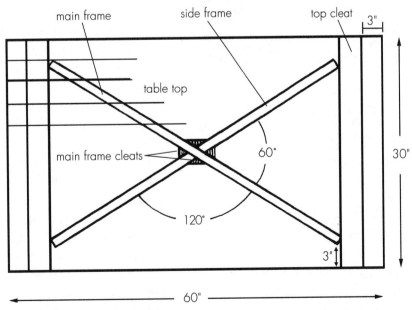

ANGLES FOR JOINING SIDE FRAMES WITH MAIN FRAME (OVERHEAD VIEW)

PROJECTS FOR THE PORCH, PATIO, DECK, & INDOORS

Projects for the Garden

ROSE ARBOR MATERIALS LIST

- 4 Posts: 4 × 4" × 8'
- 8 Arch pieces: 2 × 6 × 19", cut to fit
- 2 Upper side crosspieces: 2 × 4 × 28"
- 3 Upper arch crosspieces: 2 × 4 × 28"
- 2 Lower side crosspieces: 2 × 4 × 24"
- 8 Upper and lower horizontal lattice cleats: ¾ × ¾ × 22½"
- 8 Vertical lattice cleats: ¾ × ¾ × 63"
- 2 Treated lattice panels: 23¾ × 62½"
- 4 Angle braces: 4 × 4"

ROSE ARBOR

A ROSE ARBOR is a traditional garden fixture that can provide enjoyment for years. It can stand alone or be joined to a fence and gate such as the one shown.

Construction

This project is fairly simple to build but does require either a heavy-duty saber saw or band saw to cut the top arches. Each arch is constructed of four 2×6s doweled together.

To shape the 2×6s, you must draw a full-size pattern on a large piece of cardboard (such as a large refrigerator box). The big compass shown on page 27 is quite useful for this task as well as for future projects. Or you can make a temporary compass with a piece of string, a pencil, and a nail or tape to anchor it to the cardboard.

Using a straightedge, measure out and draw a line at the bottom of your cardboard equal to the total desired distance from one outer edge of the arch to the other (48" arch is illustrated on page 75). Position the point of the compass (or the nail attached to the piece of string) at the center of this baseline. Extend the pencil arm to the outer radius point (½ the total base length) for your desired arch.

Create a pattern for the arch, and transfer the pattern to the stock.

Cut the pattern to shape using a saber or band saw.

Set the posts in place, establish the correct post height, and level them.

Use a combination square to mark around all sides of the posts and cut to the proper height.

Cut and install the lower side crosspieces, making sure they are level in all directions.

Cut the upper side crosspieces and fasten them on the tops of the posts, leaving space at both ends for placement of arches.

73

PROJECTS FOR THE GARDEN

The arches are held together with small temporary cleats fastened to the outside, and then nailed in position on top of the posts to the upper side crosspieces. Angle braces are installed for further support.

Keeping the center point still, trace the outer arch from one end of the baseline to the other. Then position the pencil arm at the inner radius point of your arch (5½" in from outer point) and trace this arch. Divide the arch into four 45° angles by measuring with a protractor, as shown in the drawing. These four sections are cut separately and then joined by dowels. Use this arch pattern to trace and cut eight arch pieces (four for each arch), using a saber or band saw.

Use a dowelling jig to bore holes in the ends of the arch pieces. Once holes have been bored, coat each dowel and the mating ends of the pieces with resorcinol glue. Force glue into the dowel holes as well. Then tap the dowels into one piece and tap the second piece to the first. Assemble the two halves of each arch first,

Install the inner lattice cleats.

Fasten the lattice and then add the outside lattice cleats. Place the upper arch crosspieces between the arches.

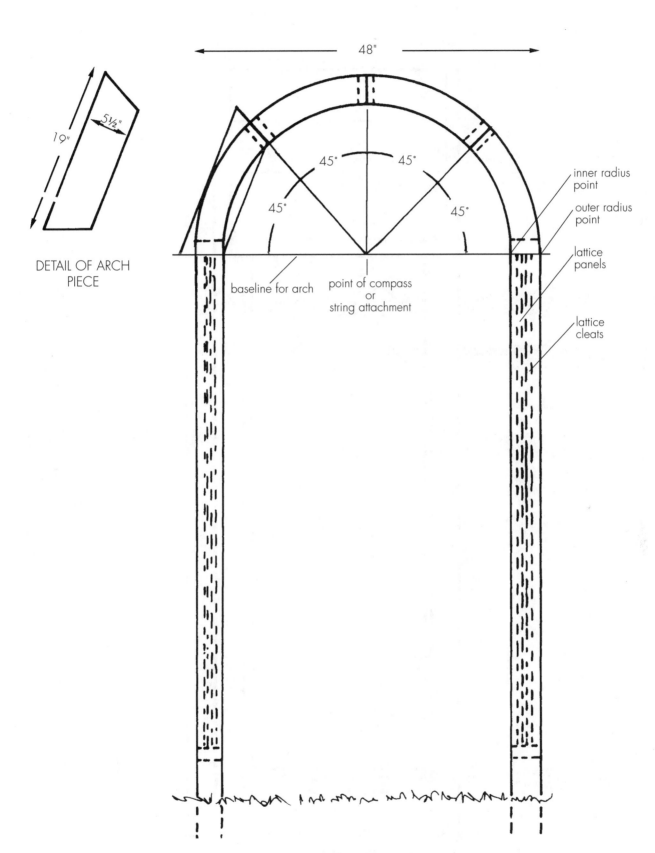

48"

19"

5½"

DETAIL OF ARCH
PIECE

45°   45°

45°   45°

inner radius
point

outer radius
point

lattice
panels

lattice
cleats

baseline for arch   point of compass
or
string attachment

FRONT ELEVATION

75

PROJECTS FOR THE GARDEN

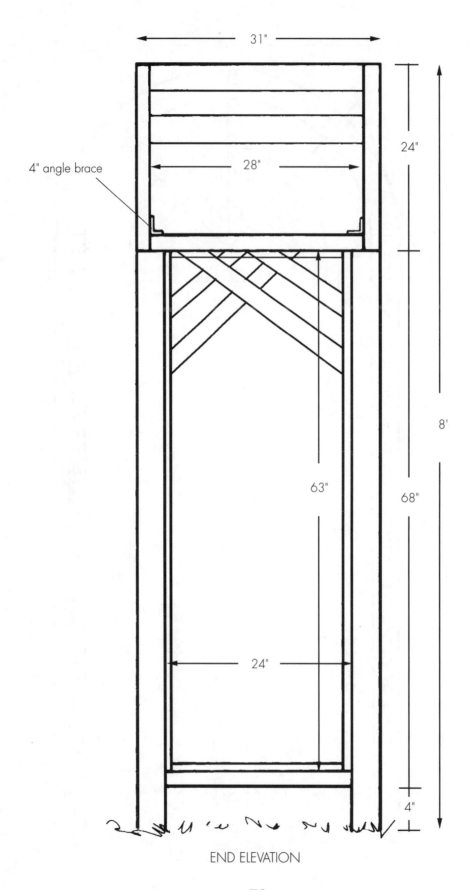

31"

24"

4" angle brace

28"

8'

68"

63"

24"

4"

END ELEVATION

64 Yard & Garden Projects You Can Build Yourself

then join them together. The completed assembly can be clamped with long pipe or bar clamps with a 2x4 straightedge across the bottom of the arch.

Once assembled, measure the distance between the bottom ends of the arches. This will be the exact distance your posts must be set. You need to create the arches first to handle any discrepancies created in the spacing.

Lay out the post spacing and dig the holes. Set the posts in the holes and embed them in concrete, making sure they are exactly plumb in all directions. Measure again to ensure that the arches will fit the posts properly. Don't worry about the height of the posts at this time beyond confirming that they are more than high enough.

Once the concrete sets, mark the desired post height on one post and use either a long level or a level placed on a straight 2x4 to mark the correct height on the remaining posts. With a carpenter's or combination square, mark around all four sides of the posts at this measurement. Then cut the posts to the correct height with a handsaw, large portable circular saw, or lightweight chain saw.

Cut the lower side crosspieces and fasten them by toenailing in place or, better yet, with 5-inch lag bolts through the posts into the ends of the crosspieces.

Next, cut the 2x4 upper side crosspieces and fasten them down on the posts with galvanized nails driven through the crosspieces into the post tops. Note that the crosspieces are cut short so the arches will fit down over the front and back of the posts.

With the upper side crosspieces in place, position the front arch and fasten 3-inch lag bolts or 16d nails through the arch bottoms into the ends of the 2x4s. Anchor the back arch in the same manner. You will probably need to brace the upper ends of the arches until the remaining braces are installed. These braces consist of 2x4s placed between the arches and anchored on their front and back with lag bolts or nails. Angle braces can also be screwed on the inside of each arch corner to help further strengthen and anchor the assembly in place.

Cut four vertical and four horizontal lattice cleats for inside ends by ripping them to size from 1-inch-thick stock using a portable circular saw with ripping guide or a table or radial arm saw. Fasten two cleats to the inside of the posts and two to the the upper and lower side crosspieces on both ends with galvanized 8d nails. Cut the lattice panels to the correct size and insert them behind the inside cleats. Thin stock like latticework will sometimes split when you hammer nails into it. Preboring holes with a bit slightly smaller than your nails prevents the problem. Cut the vertical and horizontal cleats for the outside and fasten on the outside lattice to hold the lattice panels securely in position. You can now stain, seal, or paint as desired.

The arbor is designed to support a climbing rose bush on each side. Dig the holes according to the instructions that come with the rose or refer to a good book on roses and plant accordingly. It's a good idea to use a mulch around the plants to help retain moisture and keep weeds down. I like to add an edging in a semicircle around rose bushes.

LOUNGING ARBOR

LOUNGING ARBOR MATERIALS LIST

- 4 Posts: 4 × 4 × 72" for portable unit; 4 × 4 × 96" for permanent unit
- 2 Lower end supports: 2 × 4 × 44"
- 2 Upper end rafter supports: 2 × 4 × 47"
- 1 Lower back support: 2 × 4 × 84"
- 2 Spacers: 2 × 4 × 34½", cut to fit
- 2 Rafters: 2 × 6 × 96"
- 9 Top strips: 2 × 2 × 54"
- 3 Back seat boards: 2 × 6 × 84"
- 4 Seat boards: 2 × 6 × 76"
- 1 Back lattice panel: 4 × 7'
- 2 End lattice panels: 37 × 57"

ARBORS ARE TRADITIONAL garden shelters that provide support for climbing plants such as grapes, wisteria, clematis, and climbing roses. This arbor also gives you a pleasant, shady resting spot in your garden or backyard. The comfortable bench-type seat has plenty of space for sitting and relaxing, reading a favorite book, or shelling a peck of beans. The bench is wide enough and long enough to hold a chaise lounge-style cushion or pad, which can be purchased in many garden or outdoor supply centers. The latticework sides and back and the strips on top shade you until your young plants can grow enough to cover the arbor for a more natural shade. Of course, you can also enjoy the design without plants.

The arbor shown can be constructed as a permanent structure with the posts set in concrete or anchored to concrete pads or piers. The structure can also be made portable so it

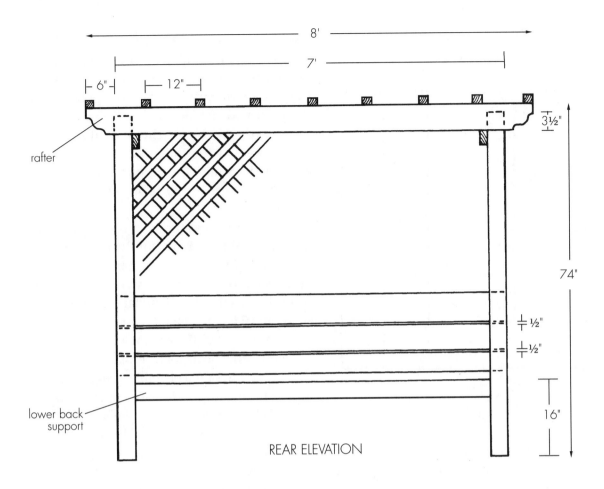

8'

7'

6" | 12"

3½"

rafter

74"

½"

½"

16"

lower back
support

REAR ELEVATION

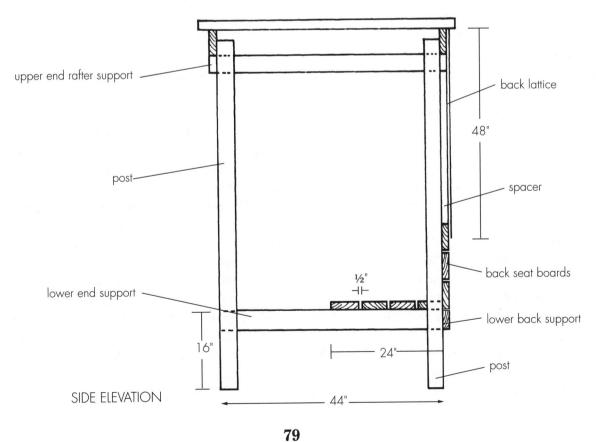

upper end rafter support

back lattice

48"

post

spacer

back seat boards

lower end support

½"

lower back support

16"

24"

post

SIDE ELEVATION

44"

79

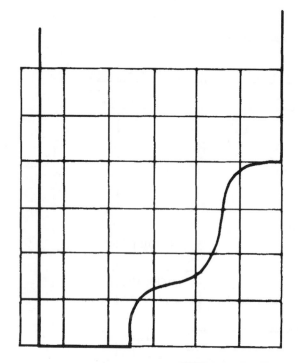

PATTERN FOR ENDS OF RAFTERS
(1 square = 1")

position a flat board against the two back stakes, place a framing square against it and use another board against that to determine the "square" location of the front posts. Once the stakes are in place, you can also measure diagonally between them to determine squareness. If the diagonal measurements are not the same, the layout is not square. Move the stakes until the measurements are the same.

With the stakes marking the post locations in position, dig the holes for the posts. The interior height of the arbor is a matter of preference. The project shown is 6 feet 2 inches from the ground to the underside of the top strips and 5 feet 8½ inches from the ground to the bottom edges of the front and rear rafters. I suggest 8-foot posts for a permanent structure and 6-foot posts for a portable structure. In the areas of the country that are colder than this part of Missouri and have a deeper frost line, you should talk with a trusted builder, lumberyard, or your Extension agent to see if you should embed your posts more deeply. If you prefer a higher clearance beneath the arbor, you'll need to purchase 10-foot poles in order to provide 7 feet of clearance to the tops of the poles (assuming a 2-foot embedment).

Set the posts in the holes, plumb both ways, and temporarily brace with 2×4s to hold the posts in position. Again, make sure they are square by running a string line around the outside edge and using a square on the string to check for squareness. Don't worry now about having all posts level across the top, but make sure their top ends are at least the proper distance above the ground level.

Once all posts are square and plumb, embed them in concrete. (See pages 162–163 for more information on embedding posts.) You may wish to stop the concrete a few inches below ground level and finish filling with top soil for a better appearance of the completed project. Or you may prefer to add gravel or other materials such as bark mulch to the inside of the arbor to cut down on mowing

can be moved if you change your landscaping. You could then even take it with you on a small trailer if you move.

The structure should be made of a long-lasting and moisture-resistant material such as pressure-treated wood. Galvanized nails should be used to fasten the structure together to prevent staining problems and provide a long-lasting construction.

Construction

You must first determine the location of your arbor if you want it to be immovable. If it will support plants such as grapes, wisteria, roses, or clematis, the arbor should be located in an area suitable for their growth.

Once you've determined the location of the arbor, drive two stakes to mark the location of the back posts. Measure and drive two stakes for the front posts as well (see drawing of side elevation). It is extremely important to get the posts positioned correctly so the arbor is square. One method to ensure squareness is to problems. In case of the latter, fill the top couple of inches of the holes in with whatever materials you've chosen.

Once the concrete has set, measure up to the correct height on the post at the highest ground level (if your ground is not level). Mark this post, then use a long level and straight board to mark this same level position on the other posts. Use a square to mark around each post at this level. Cut each post off at this height using a handsaw, portable electric saw, or chain saw.

Cut the upper end rafter supports to length and fasten one across each end of the structure at the top of the posts with 16d galvanized nails. These supports should be positioned 3½ inches below the post tops and protrude past each post 1½ inches.

Trim the front and back rafter pieces to the proper length. Enlarge the squared drawing pattern for the ends and cut to shape with a heavy-duty saber saw. Fasten these rafters across the front and back of the structure with 16d galvanized nails, resting them on the previously installed upper rafter supports.

Saw the lower end supports to the correct length and position on the inside of the end posts with their top edges approximately 16 inches above ground level. Attach with 16d galvanized nails. Cut the lower back support piece to length, remembering that it extends to the outside edge of the back posts. Place its upper edge flush with the upper edge of the two lower end supports and hammer 16d galvanized nails through the back support into both the posts and the end supports.

Cut the back seat boards to length and nail them in place, spacing them ½ inch above the lower back 2x4 support and ½ inch apart. The 2x4 spacers must be cut and fit between the back rafter and the top back seat board and nailed to the back of the back posts with 16d galvanized nails. Saw the seat boards to proper length and fasten to the lower end supports using 16d galvanized nails, spacing them ½ inch apart.

Using a table or radial arm saw or a portable circular saw with a ripping guide attachment, rip 2x6s into 2x2s (1½ inches by 1½ inches) to create the top strips. Space them 12 inches apart and attach them across the front and back rafters with 16d galvanized nails.

The back and ends of the arbor are covered with pressure-treated latticework, which comes in 4x8 sheets and can be somewhat of a hassle to handle as well as cut. Be careful, as the sheets can split or break quite easily until installed. I suggest leaning them against a flat, smooth surface to store. Cutting them to fit is a problem I've worked out because I like projects made with latticework. Position a pair of sawhorses about 6 feet apart and then place four wooden "waste" strips, at least 8 feet long, across the sawhorses to support the panels. Measure the panels for the cuts and mark across them using a long straightedge such as a 4-foot level. Cut the panels to size using a portable electric circular saw with the blade set so that it just passes through the latticework without entering the support strips too deeply. If you don't use the support strips the lattice will bend and fall, break off in pieces, or catch the saw blade and cause a dangerous kickback situation with the saw. Even with supports you have to watch that the front of the saw shoe doesn't slide under and catch on the diagonal strips as you push it forward. Don't push the saw too quickly. Go slowly and safely.

First cut the back lattice panel to fit lengthwise. It doesn't have to be ripped to fit horizontally. Fasten the latticework to the back rafter and top seat board using 4d galvanized nails along each edge to secure it solidly in place. To size the end lattice panels, carefully measure first between the end posts at both the top and bottom to ensure you get the panel cut small enough to fit in place properly. It's not very much fun to have to recut and try to slice just a tiny bit off. On the other hand, you don't want the panel so small that gaps show. Cut and fit one end panel first, then cut and fit the opposite panel. Anchor both panels with 4d galvanized nails along the top and bottom strips.

If you prefer to construct the project as a portable arbor, lay two end posts out on the ground, measure the location of the upper and lower end supports, and — after checking that the assembly is square — fasten them in place. When both ends are assembled, simply stand them on end, have a helper hold them in position, and nail on first the bottom back support piece, then the top back rafter, and finally the front rafter. Space the posts properly so the rafters extend past the posts by 6 inches on either end. Square up the assembly, then use blocks or other materials to check level across the lower supports with a 4-foot level. From here on, the assembly process is the same as for a permanent structure.

The arbor can be stained, painted, or simply given a coat of protective finish suitable for use with pressure-treated woods. Then it's time to grab some cushions and crawl in for a nap to rest after your hard work!

GRAPE TRELLIS

GRAPE VINES NEED support and must be trained for manageability and space. A wide variety of supports has evolved from simple trellises to fancy arbors. The simplest method is to erect poles and string wire between them for the grapes to vine on. The design of the trellis depends a great deal on the pruning method used to grow the grapes. In most instances one of two popular methods are used: The four-arm Kniffen system and the umbrella Kniffen system. Both utilize a trellis of posts with two wires supported by the posts. Another system utilizes three wires. The choice depends on the type of pruning management you prefer.

The trellis can be erected after the plants have grown for a year, but the best tactic is to erect the trellis when you plant the grapes. Since you'll need to dig holes for the trellis as well as the plants, you may want to rent a power post-hole digger to do everything at once. The posts can be driven in the ground with the wire attached to them, but a better looking and more permanent trellis is made from treated wood 4x4s that are 8 feet long with at least 6 feet of post above the ground. Most varieties of grapes require 8 to 10 feet of space between them.

Construction

First determine where you wish to locate the trellis, how many plants you'll need, and how much space to devote to each plant. Three vines will require a 24-foot space, and six vines need 48 feet. A very simple trellis consists of two posts set 24 feet apart with the wires strung between them. These wires will, however, tend to sag without further support and can place enough strain on the end posts to pull them out of plumb. The posts can be spaced as desired, but the optimum spacing is a post on each end and one between each grape

Grapes are supported on wires attached with screw eyes and turnbuckles to keep the wires tight.

GRAPE TRELLIS MATERIALS LIST
(for six plants and/or 48 feet)

7   Posts: 4 × 4" × 8'
3   Horizontal braces: 2 × 4" × 16'
     100' Wire, #12 gauge
4   Screw eyes
2   Turnbuckles

---

plant; 2x4 braces across the front of the posts add further support.

After determining the location of your trellis, drive stakes at each end of the site, 48 feet apart for this six-plant design. Tie a string between these stakes and measure locations for the grape plants as well as any supporting posts you desire. For six plants, I suggest five supporting posts, spaced about 8 feet apart. Drive stakes at all these locations.

Dig the post holes as well as the holes for the plants. The holes for the plants should be approximately 12 inches in circumference and 16 to 18 inches deep. If using 8-foot-long posts, the post holes should be at least 2 feet deep.

Place the posts in their holes and fill around them with concrete. The concrete should be extended aboveground and rounded off so water will run away from and not soak down around the posts.

Once the concrete has set, you can string the two wires. Anchor the wires at one end post with screw eyes. On the opposite end post the wires are held by turnbuckles fastened to screw eyes. The wires can also be placed in front of the inside support posts and held with large fencing staples. The staples should be driven in far enough to support the wires but not too tightly, as you want the wires to move freely. An alternative is to bore holes through the center of the inside support posts and simply run the wires through them. Fasten the 2x4 horizontal braces in place, making sure all posts are plumb.

Plant the grape plants in their holes according to nursery growing instructions.

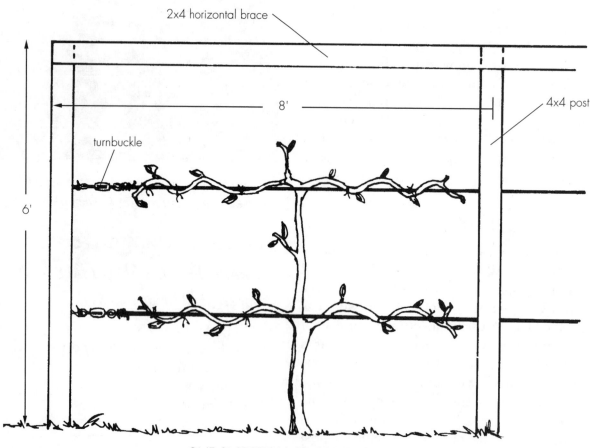

ONE 8' SECTION OF GRAPE ARBOR

64 YARD & GARDEN PROJECTS YOU CAN BUILD YOURSELF

Rose Trellises

ROSE TRELLISES have been traditional garden projects for many years. You can often drive through small towns and see roses climbing on trellises designed many years ago. Unfortunately, many old trellises haven't lasted too long, most often because of the choice of lumber. Rose trellises should be made of weather- and insect-resistant materials such as redwood, cypress, or pressure-treated lumber. I have included three popular trellis styles: a fan trellis, a simple straight trellis, and a more complicated arched trellis.

Fan Trellis

This design is one of the simplest and most fun projects in this book. A single 6-foot-long 1×6 is the only wood that's needed. The additional required materials are a handful of brads and a couple of bolts with washers. In fact, I made the trellis shown in less than an hour. If you're looking for a project you can sell at craft shows, this item has a real profit margin. With a few dollars of materials and about an hour of labor, you should be able to triple your cash investment.

This is a traditional design and will look good with any type of climbing rose. You could paint it a traditional white or even leave the wood unfinished.

The hardest part of the project is ripping the thin strips. I suggest using a portable circular saw and a ripping guide or a radial arm or table saw. I built this trellis quickly because I used a table saw. Once all the fan strips have been ripped to the proper width, lay them on edge together on a smooth, flat surface. Use two large C-clamps on the lower bottom end to bind the strips securely together. Bore two holes through the entire clamped assembly and use 2½-inch bolts with washers and nuts to fasten the lower end of the trellis together. Once the fan strips are secured, remove the clamps.

Cut the top arch piece to the proper length and lay a tape ruler on it. Beginning 1 inch from

Fan Trellis Materials List

- 5 Fan strips: ⅜ x ¾ x 72"
- 1 Top arch: ⅜ x ¾ x 50"
- 1 Center horizontal: ⅜ x ¾ x 36"
- 1 Bottom horizontal: ⅜ x ¾ x 20"
- 1 Anchoring stake: ¾ x 1¾ x 24"

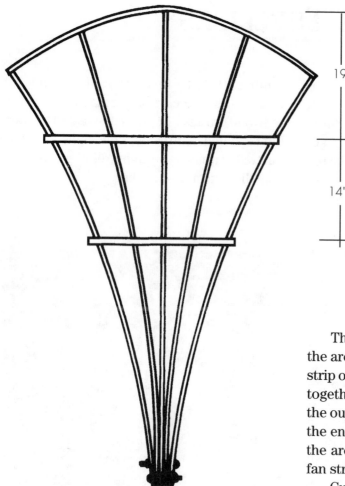

19"

14"

24"

ANCHORING
STAKE WITH
SHARPENED END

The next step is to attach the outer ends of the arch piece to the strips. Pull one outer fan strip outward and the arch down and nail them together with a 4d galvanized nail. Note that the outer fan strips are fastened 1 inch in from the ends of the arch piece to prevent splitting the arch with a nail. Attach the opposite end fan strip in the same manner.

Cut the center horizontal piece to the correct length, mark its center, and lay it in place 19 inches from the top of the center fan strip. To make sure this piece is square with the assembly, lay the long arm of a carpenter's square along the center fan strip and position the horizontal against the short arm of the square. Fasten it by driving brads down through the horizontal piece into the edges of the fan strips. Attach the shorter bottom horizontal piece the same way.

Finally, rip the anchoring stake to width and cut to length. Then make the angled ends to create a sharpened stake (see drawing). To anchor the trellis in the ground, drive the anchoring stake in your garden, leaving about 8 inches of stake protruding. Place the trellis in position against the stake, bore two holes through the bolted section of the trellis and the stake, and fasten together with 2½-inch bolts with washers and nuts.

an end, make a mark at each 1-foot increment. These mark the positions for the four fan strips.

Extend the top end of the clamped fan section out past the work surface a bit, position the center mark on the top arch piece over the center fan strip, and drive one 4d galvanized nail from the top center of the arch piece into the center fan strip. Drive the nail squarely into the center of the strip to prevent any splintering. If you have trouble getting nails through the arch piece, you can predrill the holes with a bit slightly thinner than your nails.

Grasp one of the inner fan strips, pull it outward, and push the curved arch piece down to meet it at the marked location. Fasten in place in the same manner. Go to the inside strip on the opposite side, pull it out and the arch down, and fasten them together as well.

64 Yard & Garden Projects You Can Build Yourself

STRAIGHT TRELLIS

The straight trellis is a simple and traditional trellis design. The strips are somewhat heavier for this trellis than for the fan and arched designs. Rip them to ¾-inch widths from ¾-inch stock, leaving them ¾ inch by ¾ inch. After ripping strips to the proper size, cut all pieces to the proper length.

Next, lay the long vertical strips flat on a smooth work surface and mark the locations for the horizontals at 12-inch intervals. Measure and mark locations of the long verticals on the horizontals, 3 inches from each end. Starting at either the top or bottom, place the horizontals on the marks and use a carpenter's square to make sure the assembly is square; fasten with two 4d galvanized nails through each joint. Cut the short vertical pieces and nail them in place on the horizontals in the same fashion, as shown on the drawing.

This trellis looks great painted white in the traditional manner. Drive two stakes in the ground and bolt the bottom of the outside trellis ends to them as described for the fan trellis on page 86.

on page 86.

STRAIGHT TRELLIS MATERIALS LIST

2   Long verticals: ¾ × ¾ × 78"
2   Short verticals: ¾ × ¾ × 26"
6   Horizontals: ¾ × ¾ × 30"
2   Stakes: ¾ × 1¾ × 24"

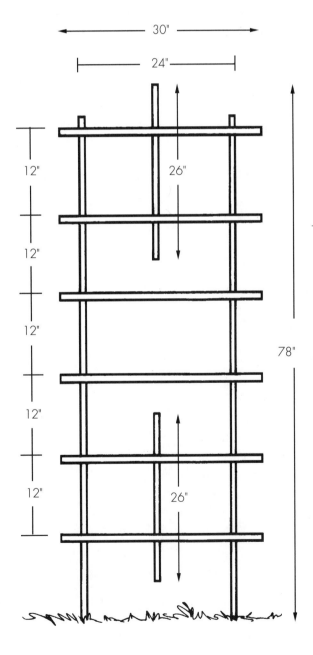

ARCHED TRELLIS

ARCHED TRELLIS
MATERIALS LIST

2   Long verticals: ⅜ × 1½ × 102"
2   Medium verticals: ⅜ × 1½ × 96"
1   Top middle vertical: ⅜ × 1½ × 24"
1   Bottom middle vertical:
    ⅜ × 1½ × 36"
4   Long horizontals: ⅜ × 1½ × 40"
6   Short horizontals: ⅜ × 1½ × 12"
1   Arch cut from ⅜" exterior plywood
4   Stakes: ¾ x 1¾ x 24"

If you prefer a sturdier and more intricate trellis than the other styles, this design is a good choice. It features an arched top, and although it appears more difficult than the fan trellis, this one is fairly easy to make. You will need a band saw, portable electric saber saw, or coping saw for some of the cuts.

Construction

Rip all pieces that need to be ripped at once. Note that these pieces are ripped from a piece of 2x stock to a ⅜-inch width. Instead of turning them on edge, place the strips flat to create the design.

With all pieces ripped to their proper widths, crosscut all pieces to their proper length. To assemble, place the verticals on a flat work surface and mark the locations for the horizontals (see drawing). After laying out locations for the verticals on all horizontals, position the horizontals across the verticals on the work surface. Make sure the assembly is square and then fasten all pieces together using three brads to each joint.

The upper arch can be made of a piece of ⅜-inch exterior plywood. Measure the distance between the upper edges of the outside verticals and use the large compass shown in Chapter 2 (or a similar tool) to draw the arch pattern on the plywood stock. Use a saber saw, coping saw, or band saw to cut the arched piece.

Nail the arched piece so that it is flat on top of the verticals, butting it down against the top horizontal. Finally, make four stakes, drive them in place, and bolt the trellis to them as described for the fan trellis on page 86.

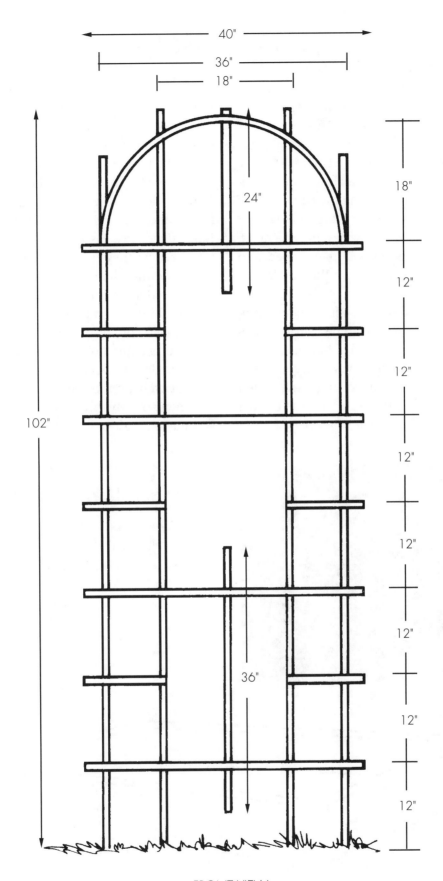

FRONT VIEW

89

PROJECTS FOR THE GARDEN

RAISED BEDS

RAISED BEDS can provide a great deal of gardening in a small space, regardless of whether you wish to grow flowers, vegetables, or herbs. In fact, herbs do especially well in raised beds. An attractive herb garden can be created by dividing the bed into sections for each type of herb. Strawberries also do extremely well in raised beds. One technique is to tier the beds, put strawberry plantings in each layer, and build in a garden sprinkler in the middle for easy watering.

Actually, raised beds are just big containers and in many ways raised bed gardening is a kind of container gardening. Raised beds offer several advantages over conventional gardening. First, beds can be built up and filled with the proper soil more easily and faster than with an in-ground plot. They can also be used to intensively space plants and produce more in a small space. Closer spacing cuts down on weeds. If built 3 to 5 feet wide — so you can reach the middle — you don't have to get into the bed to plant or weed. Without heavy objects (like gardeners) in the garden, the soil stays looser and more friable and doesn't compact. Raised beds are easier for older gardeners to tend because they can sit on the edge of the bed to work rather than having to stoop or bend as for ground-level gardens. Raised beds are often combined with modern mulches such as black plastic or plastic screening mulch, which has microscopic holes in it to let moisture in but hold down weeds.

Raised beds must have some means to contain their soil. My first raised beds were simply walnut logs left over from thinning an over-

BOX BED MATERIALS LIST

2 Sides: 2 × 6 × 72"
2 Ends: 2 × 6 × 36"

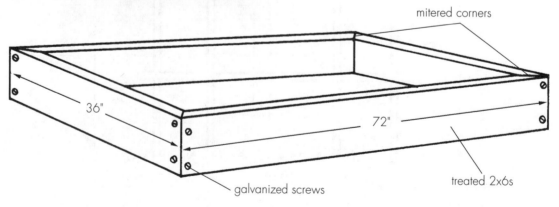

mitered corners

36"

72"

galvanized screws

treated 2x6s

grown walnut grove on our hillside farm. Concrete blocks, bricks, and rocks can be used to create a raised bed. Discarded railroad ties and preshaped pressure-treated landscaping timbers, which are specifically made for raised beds, can also be used. Such timbers are often simply laid in place or held to sloping hillsides with wooden stakes. Beds made of timbers more than one layer high can be anchored together by overlapping the corners and joining the pieces with large bolts.

Rot-resistant woods like cedar and redwood or pressure-treated 2x6s, 2x8s, or even 2x10s can also be nailed together with galvanized nails to create boxes without bottoms — "movable beds." If you're renting or may sell your property, you can simply pull these beds up and take them with you.

OCTAGONAL HERB BED MATERIALS LIST

1 Main center divider: 2 × 6 × 69"
6 Inside dividers: 2 × 6 × 33¾"
8 Outside frame pieces: 2 × 6 × 42"

LANDSCAPING TIMBER BED MATERIALS LIST

4 End timbers: 4 × 6 × 36"
6 End spacer timbers: 4 × 4 × 24"
6 Side timbers: 4 × 6 × 72"
4 Side spacer timbers: 4 × 6 × 60"
40 Galvanized aluminum spikes

42"   67½°   67½°

67½°

45°

3'

6'

OVERHEAD VIEW

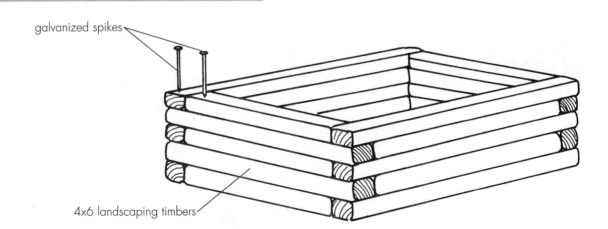

galvanized spikes

4x6 landscaping timbers

Construction

Locate the bed where it will catch full sun if possible. Mark off the size of the bed with stakes and string. Then use a shovel to dig down and remove all sod, grass, and weeds. Construct the bed itself in one of the following ways.

The quickest way to make a raised bed is to simply lay treated landscaping timbers, available at major building supply dealers, on top of each other. Overlap end joints to provide strength, as shown in the drawing of the landscaping timber bed on page 91. These joints can also be anchored more solidly with galvanized aluminum spikes driven through the corners. Treated timbers are extremely attractive, long lasting, and quite popular. Raised beds and planting terraces can hold in soil on a slope and provide space for flowers or vegetables. And they can be any size you desire.

Another method of creating extremely economical raised beds is to fasten together "boxes" of 2x6s or 2x8s, depending on the height you desire the beds. These "box beds" can be any shape: square, rectangular, or even octagonal. A three-tier bed for strawberries can be made from three stacked boxes, as illustrated. An octagonal bed with dividers is a great way of creating an herb garden with eight

THREE-TIER STRAWBERRY BED MATERIALS LIST

4 Bottom pieces: 2 × 6 × 72"
4 Center pieces: 2 × 6 × 60"
4 Top pieces: 2 × 6 × 48"

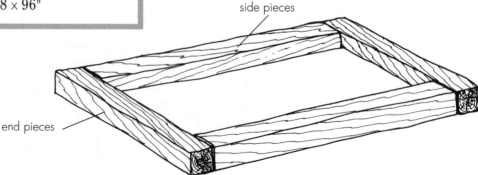

4' x 4' box

5' x 5' box

6' x 6' box

RAILROAD TIE BED MATERIALS LIST

2 End pieces: 8 × 8 × 48"
2 Side pieces: 8 × 8 × 96"

side pieces

end pieces

or nine separate planting spaces. It's important not to make your boxes so wide you can't reach across them easily from both sides, although they can be of any length. The best size I've come up with so far is 3 feet by 6 feet, which can be cut easily from 12-foot-long boards with no waste. Space the beds for a footpath or your lawn mower.

The first step in creating these beds is to determine the angles needed for the joining ends. For rectangular beds, the angles are all 90 degrees. For an octagonal bed, the angles are specified on the drawing on page 91. Next, cut the boards to the proper length and angle, which will be simpler with a stationary power saw. You can also cut boards to the correct angle with a handsaw by first using a protractor and bevel gauge to mark the correct angles and then a square to mark the top and bottom of the cuts across the boards.

Once all the boards have been cut simply fasten together with 16d galvanized nails through the joints. Large beds should be joined together on location, but smaller beds can be assembled in the shop and carried to the site. Once the bed is in position, level it in all directions and make sure it is in the correct shape and the joints are solidly anchored together. Adding 2x2 corner blocks to the inside of the joints can strengthen the corners a great deal.

Raised beds can be made by simply mitering the corners of 2×6s and fastening them together with 16d galvanized nails.

Once the sides are completed, fill your beds with compost.

SOIL FOR YOUR RAISED BEDS

Naturally, raised beds will only produce well if the proper growing medium is used. You can simply dump soil into the beds once they're in position, but the best results require a little more effort in initial creation to cut down on wasted time and problems later. Begin by laying out the location of the bed. Then remove the turf and grass from the area. Dig down about 2 feet and turn the soil over as you go. Level the area as much as possible and set the bed in place. Fill with soil, compost, and manure, spreading and mixing them together well. Wood ashes and rock minerals can also be added for extra growing "oomph." Once the growing medium is in place, use a board to level the surface and you're ready to plant. Incidentally, one tactic I discovered last summer for quick and simple watering of some annuals and some leeks and dill I had in an herb bed was to run a soaker irrigation hose across the top of the bed once planted. Strawberries do extremely well in this type of bed.

COLD FRAME/HOT BED

A COLD FRAME MAKES gardening more productive by extending your growing season, particularly when raising herbs and salad greens. Basically, cold frames are raised beds with a "lid" that allows sunlight to filter in but keeps out the cold. Last year I constructed several raised beds early in the spring and used them throughout the summer months. In the fall I added a cold frame top to one for winter gardening. The cold frame shown utilized scraps of Filon fiberglass greenhouse panels from a project in my book *How to Build Small Barns and Outbuildings*. However, you can simply purchase the small amount of glazing needed for this project.

For longevity and good looks, use pressure-treated materials. Make sure the label states that the product is acceptable for ground-contact use. By the same token, fasteners should be of galvanized metal to prevent rust stains and to prolong the life of the project.

A cold frame will only produce well if the soil is appropriate. Refer to the raised beds projects on page 93 for suggestions on preparing a good growing medium.

Enclosing the box bed with a lid of glass or fiberglass allows the sun to heat the interior. Lids can be as simple or fancy as you desire. Discarded wooden storm windows or recycled window sashes can work as the top, or you can create your own (as shown) using double-strength glass or special fiberglass greenhouse panels. A cold frame can be constructed as a permanent stand-alone structure, attached to the south side of a building, or even built as a portable unit if bolts are used in the corners so they can easily be disassembled and moved.

The main difference between a cold frame and a raised bed is that the planting surface must be far enough below the top of the frame to allow plants such as lettuce room to grow properly. Usually, you need a depth of at least 6 to 8 inches. Construction of the basic box for this project is the same as for bed boxes. The cold frame should be set in the ground somewhat to prevent cold from seeping in around the edges, or you can set it on ground level (after preparing the soil in the same manner as for the box bed) and then add soil around the edges to create a "berm" to hold in heat and keep out cold.

Construction

First create the box, adding mitered corner blocks to strengthen the construction (see the instructions for box beds on page 90). Prepare the soil and build or position the box in place over the prepared bed. Then construct the top lid of your choice.

To make the top pictured, join the four frame pieces with cross lap joints. To form a lap joint, measure the width and depth of the piece that will be lapping the piece you are cutting first. In this case, the area of wood you will be removing from each piece will measure ¾ inch by 1½ inches by 1½ inches. Make the first cut with a hand or electric saw across the piece

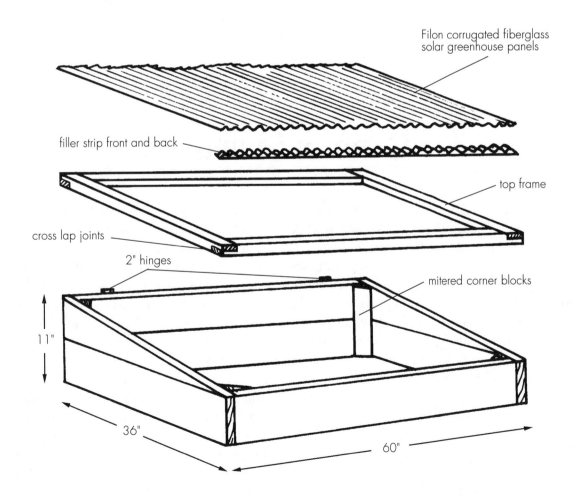

Filon corrugated fiberglass solar greenhouse panels

filler strip front and back

top frame

cross lap joints

2" hinges

mitered corner blocks

11"

36"

60"

1½ inches from the end, remembering to limit the depth of the cut to only ¾ inch. Next, make three or four identical and evenly spaced cuts between your first mark and the end of the

piece. Remove the waste carefully with a sharp chisel, pushing by hand from the end and without using a mallet or hammer. After cutting the piece's mate, trim the joint to fit with a chisel if necessary. Note that you can also use a dado blade on a table or radial arm saw to remove the waste wood in a number of quick passes.

To seal off the edges of the corrugated fiberglass panels, I used a strip of ¾-inch by 1-inch board on which I had traced the panel ends. The strips were then cut to shape using a band saw; a portable saber saw or coping saw could also be used. Fasten the shaped strips to the frame and greenhouse panel using brads. The top frame can be left unattached, but it is more efficient if it is hinged at the back with butt hinges. You'll also need a prop board or a stick to hold the top partially open to allow air circulation to cool down the unit during warm days but still close the frame at night to keep in the heat.

HOT BED

You can easily change a cold frame into a hot bed that can be used to start seedlings in cold climates. At one time horse manure — a very "hot" manure — was dug down below the planting soil to provide the heat. These days special electric heating cables do the job much easier and with a lot less hassle and smell. Make sure your heating cable specifies it is for buried use. To install a heating cable, remove the soil below the bottom edge of the frame and insert a 2-inch layer of sand. Lay the cable over the sand and add soil on top.

GARDEN SUPPORTS

GARDENING SUPPORTS PROVIDE a great deal of growing area in a small space. In fact, plants such as cucumbers, peas, pole beans, raspberries, blackberries, and even many types of tomatoes take up less room and do better when grown vertically on supports. Fruits and vegetables often have less of a tendency to rot because they're not lying on the ground and they're easier to pick, and larger crops can be produced because the flowers are more exposed. A wide variety of fences, trellises, stakes, and supports can be used. Many types of supports can be purchased, but you can build your own to suit your needs.

The simplest kind of garden support is a fence. An existing wooden fence can be used

as a vertical garden by fastening hog or woven wire to one side. If you don't have an appropriate existing fence, however, you can easily make your own. Although the details can vary, the posts should be a rot-resistant material like redwood, cedar, or pressure-treated wood. For berries, the posts should protrude 6 feet above ground level and be embedded 2 feet deep with #9 wires stapled to them.

A fence for growing cucumbers and other vining plants can consist of hog or woven wire stapled to the posts. For portable fencing, use steel posts and wire the fencing materials to the posts so the fencing sections can be taken down easily at the end of the season or taken with you if you move.

64 YARD & GARDEN PROJECTS YOU CAN BUILD YOURSELF

GARDEN PANELS

Peas and cucumbers grow well on a section of garden panels, which are made of 12-foot-long treated 1x3s covered with chicken wire. We even used three of the panels to create a portable dog pen when we acquired a new Irish setter puppy last spring, and we moved the panels around the yard as needed until she got big enough for the regular dog pen.

GARDEN PANELS MATERIALS LIST

- 2 Horizontals: 1 × 3 × 144"
- 3 Verticals: 1 × 3 × 48"
  Chicken wire: 48" × 144"

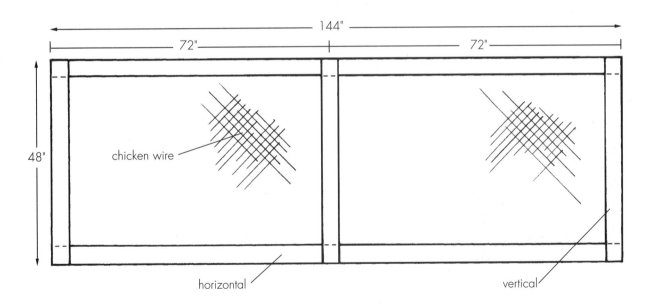

Trellis Container

Trellis Container
Materials List

2 Box ends: 1 × 12 × 16½"
2 Box sides: 1 × 12 × 48"
2 Uprights: 2 × 2 × 74"
5 Horizontals: 1 × 2 × 50"
1 Bottom: 1 × 16½ × 46½"

An excellent gardening technique is to combine a plant container with a trellis or fence. A trellis container is simply a box with a trellis anchored to the back, which is great for a few beans or cucumbers. You can also use a raised bed with a fence erected along one side. Either method provides a lot more planting space from the same raised bed or container.

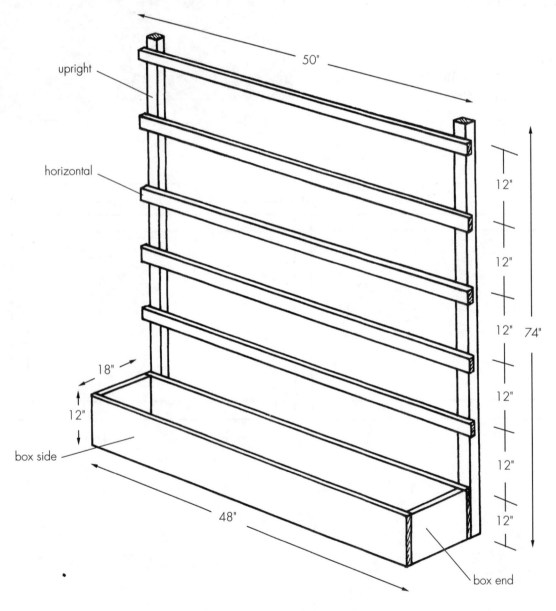

upright

horizontal

50"

12"

12"

12" 74"

12"

12"

12"

18"

12"

box side

48"

box end

A-Frame Bean Support

Pole beans require tall supports. Even though you can purchase them, you can readily construct your own with either a tepee of 2×2 posts or a portable 2×2 A-frame-style version. The supports are bolted and wired together to create a support frame. Galvanized 4d nails are spaced along the bottom and top frame and twine threaded around the nails for the plants to vine on. The entire unit can be quickly erected and disassembled.

A-Frame Bean Support Materials List

3 Horizontal supports: 2 × 2" × 16'
6 Uprights: 2 × 2" × 6'
2 Diagonal supports: 2 × 2" × 18'
   (only one shown in drawing)
6 Bolts, washers, and nuts: ⅜ × 4"
   Wire and twine

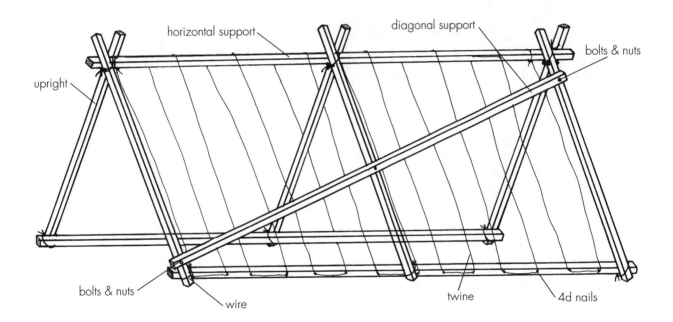

horizontal support   diagonal support   bolts & nuts

upright

bolts & nuts   wire   twine   4d nails

BEAN TOWER

This bean tower is very portable. Three sides are covered with twine, the beans are planted against these sides. The fourth side is left open so you can step or reach inside the tower to pick beans.

BEAN TOWER MATERIALS LIST

  4 Uprights: 2 × 2 × 96"
  4 Top crosspieces: 2 × 2 × 12"
  4 Bottom crosspieces: 2 × 2 × 48"
  3 Diagonal braces: 2 × 2" × 9', cut to fit
 28 Screws: #10 2¼"
     Ball of string

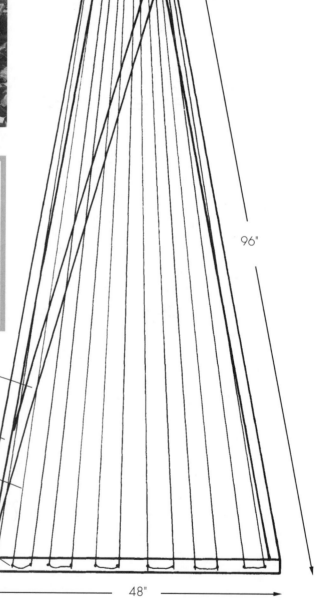

12"

top crosspiece

96"

diagonal brace

upright

twine

nails

bottom crosspiece

48"

Construction

Begin by ripping the four upright pieces, since the 2×2s (really 1½ inches by 1½ inches) are ripped from 2×4s. Rip the top and bottom crosspieces as well.

Cut the top and bottom crosspieces to their proper length, and partially drive nails in place on three top and three bottom pieces to hold the string. Then lay out one side using two uprights and a top and bottom crosspiece. Place one #10 2¼-inch screw through each end of the crosspieces into the upright. Assemble another side in the same manner. Then place these assemblies upright on a smooth, flat surface and fasten a top and bottom crosspiece to connect the two side frames. You'll probably have to have some help to hold the frames upright as you get them fastened together. Attach the opposite top and bottom unnailed crosspieces in the same manner.

Next, stand the assembly upright and shift it around until it sits squarely. Drive a second #10 2¼-inch screw through each joint to secure it further. Diagonal braces can be used to ad-ditionally strengthen the assembly. Braces are added on only three sides to leave one side open for access to the interior.

After winding string around the galvanized 4d nails, position the bean support in your garden. Mulching the inside keeps weeds down and helps to hold in moisture.

Once you've set your bean tower in place, prepare the soil around it for planting.

TOMATO SUPPORTS

SOME TOMATO VARIETIES don't require support; the determinate or "bush" types stop growing at a certain height. Most tomatoes, however, require support. If allowed to sprawl on the ground, the plants will take up a lot of space, the tomatoes will rot, and they'll be hard to pick. When staked, the fruit will ripen earlier and the tomatoes will usually be larger than those that are left to sprawl. It's also much easier to control disease and to find and pick off insects such as tomato worms when plants are staked. I've even tried mulching unsupported plants with straw, but the results are usually the same: fewer tomatoes and a bigger patch. For those varieties that do require support, there are three typical methods: stakes, trellises, and cages. The choice you make depends on the number of tomato plants you raise and the time and money you want to put into the supports. Don't let the initial cost be the only consideration; sturdy, well-made supports will last a long time if cared for.

Tomatoes that are supported require mulch to keep weeds down and to retain moisture in the soil, which is important because they are more exposed to wind and heat.

IMPROVED TOMATO STAKES

IMPROVED TOMATO STAKES
MATERIALS LIST

1 stake per plant: 2 x 2" x 72"
12 to 13 per stake: 16d galvanized
    nails (or any size)

The simplest method of supporting tomatoes is to tie them to stakes since the materials cost and initial labor are insignificant. All that is needed is to drive the stakes in the garden. Staking tomatoes, however, requires more effort as the season progresses since you will have to continually retie the plants to the stakes as they grow. This process is time consuming and can often bruise or even break plants.

Tomato stakes can be made of any number of items. A favorite tactic in my part of the country where there are numerous sawmills is to purchase slabs or trimmings from the sides of the logs cut at sawmills and rip these slabs into tomato stakes. For the design I've outlined here, ripping 2x pressure-treated lumber into 2x2s works well.

Stakes can be as high (or, rather, as long) as you choose. It's mighty hard, however, to drive the longer stakes into the ground. I tried with a stepladder and a post maul one year and nearly broke my neck. If the stakes are no larger than 2 inches in diameter, they can be driven with a steel post driver, which makes the job quick and easy. The stakes sold at garden supply stores are usually 4 to 5 feet high. In most instances 6-foot-high stakes are better, as they can be driven 1 to 1½ feet in the ground and leave 4½ to 5 feet of exposed support. Even better for the huge plants I normally grow is an 8-foot stake driven 2 feet in the ground.

The bottom ends of stakes should be sharpened. You can do this with a hatchet, but it is easier with a handsaw or portable circular saw. One basic feature of my improved stakes is any size of galvanized nails driven into all sides of the stake. These prevent the ties for the tomato plants from sliding down the stakes. The stakes should be driven in the ground at the same time you put the plants in. I placed mine about 4 to 6 inches away from the plants.

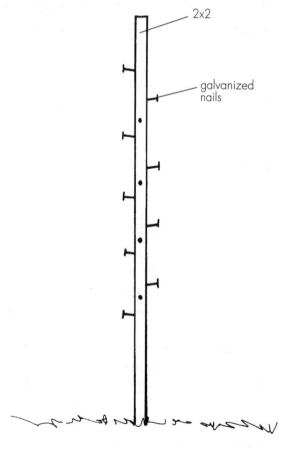

2x2

galvanized nails

TOMATO CAGES

Wooden tomato stakes are easy to form but can be hard to use, especially if you have a lot of fast-growing plants. Tomato cages are harder to make, but they are more durable and require less maintenance during the growing season. Although cages can be purchased, I suggest you make up your own from woven wire. Cut the wire into sections large enough to form into circles about 2 feet in diameter. Unfortunately, wind is a big problem for these cages and easily blows the cages — and the tomatoes — over. In some cases, even the weight of the plants can pull the cages over. How can you prevent these problems? One solution is to use wire "stakes." However, my father created an easier system.

For years I've used handmade wire cages held in place with a treated 2×2 running through the top wire openings of each cage and supported by a few steel fence posts. We usually raise a hundred plants every season in this manner. I dig the holes for the tomatoes with two tomato plants to a cage, put in the plants, then lay a soaker hose along the centerline of plants. The soaker hose and the area around the plants is then covered with straw mulch. Finally, the wire baskets are positioned

TOMATO CAGES MATERIALS LIST
(for 28–30 cages, or 72 feet)

1 Roll woven wire, 4' high
6 Steel posts
4 Top holding poles: 2 × 2" × 16'
1 Top holding pole: 2 × 2" × 8'
   Wire to hold the 2×s in place

down over the plants and mulch and held in place with the top holding poles running through the top of all the cages. To water, simply turn on the hose. The mulch keeps the weeds down and helps hold the moisture in. Black plastic mulch can also be used. We produce bushels of tomatoes in this manner.

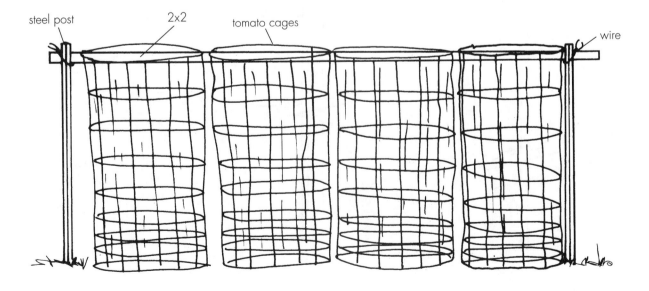

steel post   2x2   tomato cages   wire

103

Tomato Trellis

Tomatoes can also be grown on a trellis. Trellises are attractive — sometimes formal — and require a bit more work and materials than cages. I have plans for several different types of trellises. A typical trellis (not pictured) consists of 2x4 stakes or metal fence posts spaced about 5 feet apart. Next, #12 wire is fastened to the posts by wiring around 8d nails driven into the wooden stakes or by using twist-wires to hold the wire securely on the metal posts. There should be three wires approximately 1 foot apart, with the first about 1 foot off the

ground. As the plants grow, you'll need to tie the stems to the wires and weave them around the wires. Once the plants reach the upper wire, cut the tops off so they'll produce more fruit and less leafy plant growth. You will probably have to continually tie and interweave the plants to keep the vines well supported when heavy with fruit.

A friend of mine grows tomatoes on a more complicated type of trellis. This trellis consists of wooden 2x4 stakes with crossbars nailed approximately 2 feet off the ground and 2 feet above that (as illustrated). The number and spacing of the crossbars can be adjusted for the size of your particular tomato plant variety. The stakes are driven into the ground at approximately 5-foot intervals, with the tomatoes planted in a row between them.

String wire across the outer ends of the top of each crossbar, held in position with twist-wires. The plants will grow up through the framework, supported by the crossbars and wire. They still require frequent tying with this type of trellis.

Tomato Trellis Materials List

Stakes: 2 x 4" x 6'
Crossbars: 2 x 2 x 24", 2 per stake
Supports: #12 wire

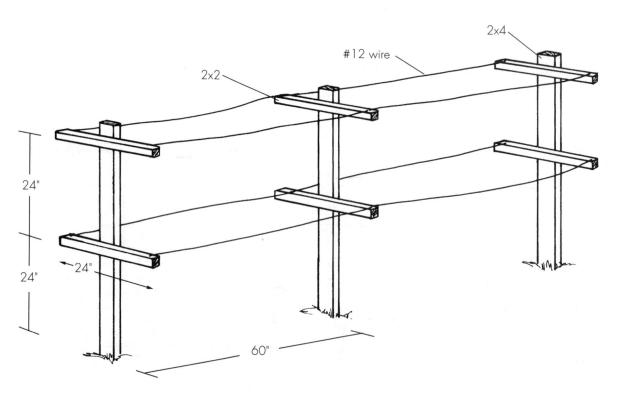

Greenhouses

PORTABLE SEED-STARTING GREENHOUSE

GREENHOUSES ARE a lot of fun, and we use ours for an assortment of home-started flowers and vegetables. A permanent, year-round greenhouse is expensive to build and to keep up. The structure shown, however, is on skids and is portable. If you decide you don't want it in a specific area, you can pull it somewhere else. Or if you happen to move, you can take the greenhouse with you. With some effort, it will fit on a flatbed trailer.

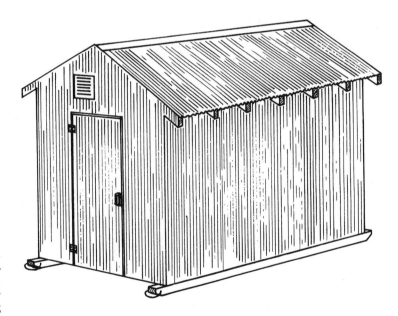

It is designed as a seasonal house without additional heating or fancy ventilation. Hinged and screened openings in the upper part of both ends allow for cross ventilation. Without additional doors or windows, it is relatively economical and extremely easy to build. It's even a good project for a beginning "building builder." With lots of water inside and outside the greenhouse, the entire structure should be constructed of pressure-treated materials.

Construction

1. The greenhouse rests on two 4-inch by 6-inch skids; begin by cutting these pieces to 13-foot lengths. The fronts and backs of the skids should have a 45-degree bevel so they don't dig in when the structure is pulled. Bore a ¾-inch hole at the front and back of each skid. Loops of #9 wire are fastened in each of these holes to hook up a chain to move the building.

2. Position the skids on a flat surface, spacing them 8 feet apart. Cut the end floor joists and anchor them in place with 8-inch lag screws in counterbored holes down through their tops into the skids. Cut the side floor joists and anchor them with lag screws into the skids as well. Drive lag screws through the end floor joists into each side floor joist. It's extremely important to make sure the structure is square at this point. Use a carpenter's square to achieve squareness initially, then measure diagonally from corner to corner. If the measurements are the same, the structure is square. If not, shift the corners until the measurements are correct.

3. Once the unit is square, add the inside floor joists between the side floor joists. Nail solidly with 16d galvanized nails. Position the ¾-inch plywood floor and fasten down to the floor joists with 8d ring-shank nails.

4. The remainder of the structure is framed like most other wood-framed structures. Construct the front end wall first by cutting the end floor plate to length and attaching it to the end floor joists by nailing through the floor decking. Leave it full length; you can cut between the door frames after the wall is installed. Cut the end lower top plate and then the end and door frame studs to length. Nail these studs between the plates at the correct positions (see front end elevation drawing) with 16d nails. Cut the mid-wall horizontals to their proper size and nail them between the studs at the proper distance.

5. The door utilizes a doubled 2x4 header. Cut the 2x4s to the proper length, nail them together, and then position them between the door uprights; nail down from the end lower top plate into the door header with 16d nails. Cut the door jack studs that support the header and nail them into the door uprights. Stand this end assembly up in place, plumb it, and then

---

PORTABLE SEED-STARTING GREENHOUSE MATERIALS LIST

2	Skids: 4 × 6" × 13'
2	Side floor joists: 2 × 6" × 11'9"
2	End floor joists: 2 × 6" × 8'
5	Inside floor joists: 2 × 6" × 7'9"
3	Floors: ¾" plywood × 4 × 8'
2	End floor plates: 2 × 4" × 8'
2	Side floor plates: 2 × 4" × 11'5"
27	Studs: 2 × 4" × 6'10½"
2	Door jack studs: 2 × 4" × 6'8"
2	End upper top plates: 2 × 4" × 7'5"
2	End lower top plates: 2 × 4" × 8'
2	Side upper top plates: 2 × 4" × 12'
2	Side lower top plates: 2 × 4" × 11'5"
7	Lookouts: 2 × 4 × 28", cut to fit
2	Door headers: 2 × 4 × 39"
1	Horizontal and miscellaneous framing: 2 × 4" × 36', cut to fit
14	Rafters: 2 × 4 × 66", cut to fit
1	Ridgeboard: 2 × 4" × 12'
8	Purlins: 2 × 4" × 12'
7	Collar ties: 2 × 4" × 4', cut to fit
23	Filon greenhouse panels: 36" × 8'
24	Filon greenhouse panels: 24" × 8'
1	12' White ridge trim

DOOR
2	Horizontals: 2 × 2 × 36"
2	Verticals: 2 × 2 × 79"
2	Butt hinges: 3"
	Door latch
2	Vents: automatic or fan vents (Purchase these first and then frame the vent openings to fit.)

---

64 YARD & GARDEN PROJECTS YOU CAN BUILD YOURSELF

brace with 2×4s at the sides nailed through the end floor plate, the plywood floor, and down into the end floor joist. Construct the rear wall in the same manner. Space the studs on 2-foot centers. Stand frame up and brace and anchor it.

6. Construct the side walls and stand them in position. Fasten the sides to the end walls with 16d nails from the side wall studs into the end wall studs. Nail down through the floor plates and decking into the end floor joists. Install the side upper top plates, allow-

ing them to overlap the end lower top plates. Nail down through the top plates and into the studs of the end walls. Then cut the end upper top plates to fit and fasten them between the side upper top plates.

7. Now you're ready for the roof framing. Cut the rafters to their correct length and shape (see box on page 153). Cut the center ridgeboard to length. Nail a center end lookout on each end of the building and tack-nail the ridgeboard down on each lookout. Position two end rafters and nail each in place by

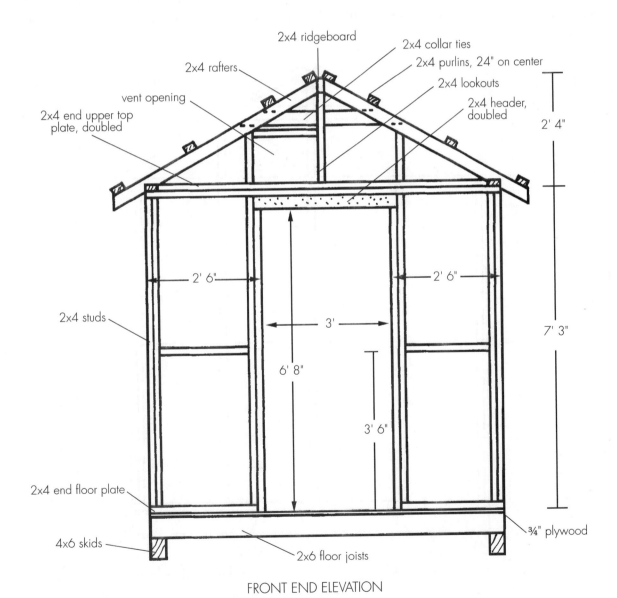

FRONT END ELEVATION

toenailing into the ridgeboard and down through the rafter into the upper top plates. Fasten the opposite end rafters in the same manner. Next, install the rafters between the ends. Cut the purlins to length and nail them down on the rafters. Then cut the lookouts to length, notch them to fit behind the end rafters, and nail between the rafters and the upper top plates. Cut two crossbraces and nail them into a set of rafters down on the top plate. These can also act as hanging basket hangers as well as provide bracing at the top to prevent the building side walls from expanding outward. Cut the collar ties to fit across the rafter tops and fasten them to each rafter. Finally, cut and

fasten the framing pieces for the vent doors on either end.

8. I suggest you cover the entire structure with Filon greenhouse panels. They have a prismatic surface that breaks up the sun's rays and provides a diffuse light to promote uniform plant growth. The panels are made of fiberglass and are shatter resistant.

9. If you use these or similar panels, cover the ends of the building first, cutting around the door and the frames for the upper vents. Fasten the panels with metal roofing nails utilizing compression washers. These must be driven with just the proper amount of pressure to prevent smashing — or even crack-

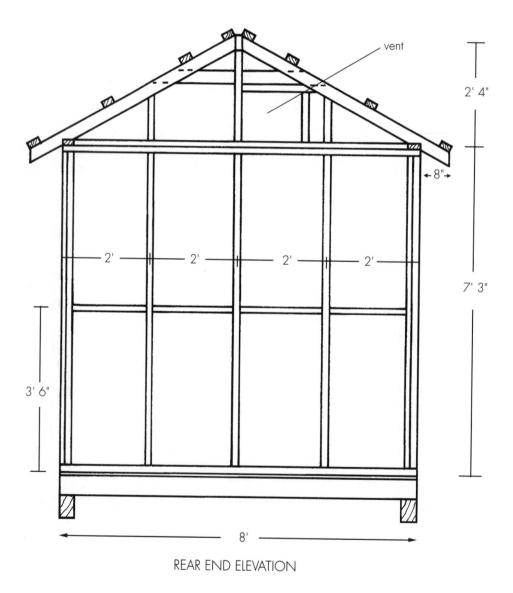

REAR END ELEVATION

64 YARD & GARDEN PROJECTS YOU CAN BUILD YOURSELF

ing—the plastic panels but still provide a snug, waterproof fit. Special wooden filler strips are available with the panels that are placed behind the panels to help fasten them and insulate gaps. Once the ends are finished, install the paneling around the sides as well.

10. Fasten the roof panels down over the purlins and extend their edges over the ends by about 1 inch. Finish off the top ridge using a section of white ridge trim normally used for metal roofs. Finally, caulk all open joints, corners, under the roof at the ends and sides, and other seams with a clear caulk such as Magic Seal.

11. Cut the interior frame members for the upper ventilation openings to size, cover

them with plastic, and hinge with butt hinges on one side. Add one eye and hook for closure and another set to keep the doors open when needed.

12. Construct the framework for the entry door from the horizontal and vertical 2x2s. Cover with greenhouse panels; add the filler trim, the top and bottom, and the center horizontal. The door is hung using butt hinges mortised into the sides of the door frame and the door. A hook and eye completes the construction.

13. If the greenhouse heats up too much, a vent fan can be positioned in one of the end ventilator frame openings.

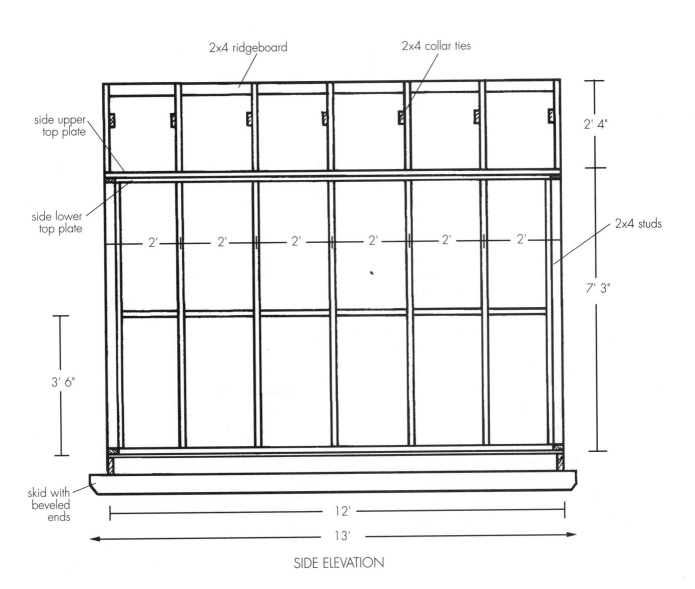

SIDE ELEVATION

Add-on Greenhouse

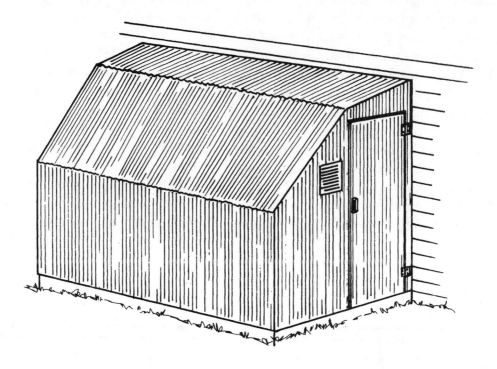

ADD A GREENHOUSE to your home for growing vegetables and flowers conveniently and extending the growing season. This add-on greenhouse can be separate from your home interior and accessed through an outside door, or you can cut a door from the house into the greenhouse. You can even open your house wall and create a solar room, although that requires a great deal more construction expertise, a different wall covering, and more money than this simple design. The basic construction strategies for a solar room, however, are the same. And this design is quite easy to build, even if you haven't attempted major carpentry before.

The add-on greenhouse should be constructed of pressure-treated wood. I also suggest you cover it with Filon greenhouse panels. Their prismatic designs reflect and diffuse the light throughout the structure for more even lighting. This design is relatively inexpensive because of the choice of materials and the

need to build only three sides. Add-on greenhouses are usually a bit stronger than freestanding greenhouses because they are anchored firmly to the house.

If you prefer to have a solar room, the framing materials should be more "finished" in appearance; wood such as heart redwood or western white cedar would be a good choice. The covering could be double-strength glass or special greenhouse panels glazed in place. The latter is very labor intensive and difficult to install, and requires a great deal more maintenance since the caulk eventually dries and the wood shrinks away from the joints. You'll constantly be replacing caulk or repainting. My first greenhouse was a glazed double-strength glass affair with the glass set in rabbets in all joints.

The most important requirement for an add-on greenhouse is a flat, obstruction-free wall on which to attach it. If possible the wall should face south or nearly so. Our first greenhouse actually faced east and it did quite well, although we had to continually move plants to prevent them from becoming leggy.

Your greenhouse could be constructed on treated timbers placed in the ground with gravel poured between the timbers. A poured concrete slab floor, however, is better for several reasons. First, it provides a stable and level floor on which to build. Second, it will stay level, whereas timbers may sink and tilt in time. Third, it's also easier to clean a concrete floor, and you'll always have dirt and debris to clean from your greenhouse. But most importantly, the mass of concrete acts as a heat sink that gathers daytime heat and releases it slowly at night. This design utilizes a slab only. In some parts of the country you may need to pour a footing around the slab edges to prevent frost heaving, so check with your local county Extension agent or a good building supply dealer before building.

Construction

1. The first step is to determine the location on your house wall for the greenhouse. Measure and mark the end locations then, using a 4-foot level or a plumb bob held above the marks, determine plumb and the exact location of the end walls. Mark these lines with a heavy pencil on the house siding.

2. Measure outward from the wall on each end the distance the greenhouse is to extend (in this case 6 feet). Place a stake with a nail partially driven in the center top at each approximate location. To assure the structure is square, measure diagonally from each stake to the end location on the house. If the measurements are the same, the building is square. If they are not the same, shift the stakes until the measurements are identical.

3. Once you have established the exact outside corners of the greenhouse, run a string line from nails driven in the house siding where the structure attaches across the nails on the stakes. Use a plumb bob to determine

ADD-ON GREENHOUSE MATERIALS LIST

FRONT
- 1 Bottom plate: 2 x 4 x 31½"
- 1 Center plate: 2 x 4 x 30"
- 2 Vent opening pieces: 2 x 4 x 18", cut to fit
- 2 Door headers: 2 x 4 x 39"
- 3 Short studs: 2 x 4 x 45"
- 1 Rear stud: 2 x 4 x 92½"
- 2 Door support studs: 2 x 4 x 80"
- 1 Center stud: 2 x 4 x 82"
- 1 Lower rafter: 2 x 4 x 50"
- 1 Upper rafter: 2 x 4 x 42"

BACK
- 1 Bottom plate: 2 x 4 x 72"
- 1 Front center plate: 2 x 4 x 30"
- 1 Middle center plate: 2 x 4 x 12"
- 1 Rear center plate: 2 x 4 x 22½"
- 2 Top plates: 2 x 4 x 39"
- 1 Rear stud: 2 x 4 x 92½"
- 1 Center stud: 2 x 4 x 82"
- 3 Tall studs: 2 x 4 x 80½"
- 3 Short studs: 2 x 4 x 45"
- 1 Lower rafter: 2 x 4 x 50"
- 1 Upper rafter: 2 x 4 x 42"
- 2 Vent opening pieces: 2 x 4 x 18", cut to fit

SIDE
- 1 Lower plate: 2 x 4" x 11'5"
- 1 Center plate: 2 x 4" x 11'5"
- 7 Studs: 2 x 4 x 45"
- 6 Upper front braces: 2 x 4 x 22½", cut to fit
- 1 Sill plate: 2 x 4" x 11'9"

TRUSSES
- 5 Lower truss rafters: 2 x 4 x 50", cut to fit
- 5 Upper truss rafters: 2 x 4 x 42", cut to fit
- 12 Truss plates: ⅜ plywood x 6 x 12"
- 4 Filon greenhouse solar panels: 36" x 8' for ends
- 9 Filon greenhouse panels: 12" x 8' for side

Door hardware, hinges, and lock

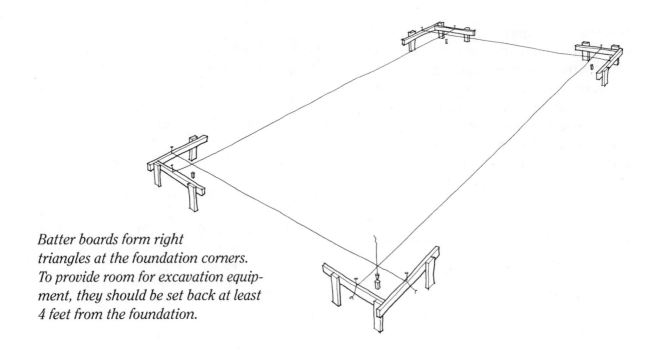

Batter boards form right triangles at the foundation corners. To provide room for excavation equipment, they should be set back at least 4 feet from the foundation.

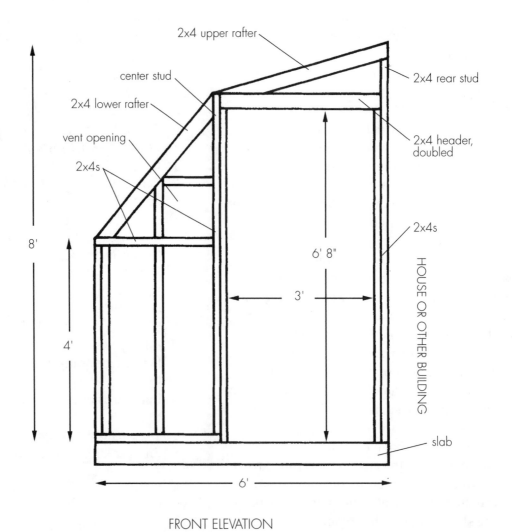

2x4 upper rafter

center stud

2x4 lower rafter

vent opening

2x4s

2x4 rear stud

2x4 header, doubled

2x4s

8'

4'

6' 8"

3'

HOUSE OR OTHER BUILDING

slab

6'

FRONT ELEVATION

the exact placement of the corner stakes. Set up batter boards placed at each corner, at least 4 feet outside the structure perimeter as shown in the drawing. Establish the building outline with string fastened to nails driven in the top of the batter boards. The string can be removed for excavation work and other tasks and then be replaced to give an accurate, consistent outline for the building. Batter boards are important to have when you might destroy stakes that mark the precise corners of a building.

4. Using the string lines as guides, mark these boundaries and dig down below the turf about 4 inches through the whole area and extending 1 foot outside the boundary lines in all directions and up to the house foundation. Again, in some colder areas you will need a different type of foundation.

5. The next step is to create the form to hold the slab with 2xs. Nail them to stakes driven in the ground at the corners and where the slab will meet the house foundation. Between corners, space stakes every couple of feet. The form should slope away from the house foundation about ½ inch to allow for drainage. The form should, however, be level from side to side.

6. Once the form is solidly in place, 2 inches of gravel should be poured in and raked out smooth. Cut strips of welded reinforcing wire and lay them over the gravel.

7. The next step is to pour the concrete. Although it may seem daunting, pouring a slab of this size is not particularly complicated even though it can be hard work. A pour of this size is best done with ready-mix concrete delivered

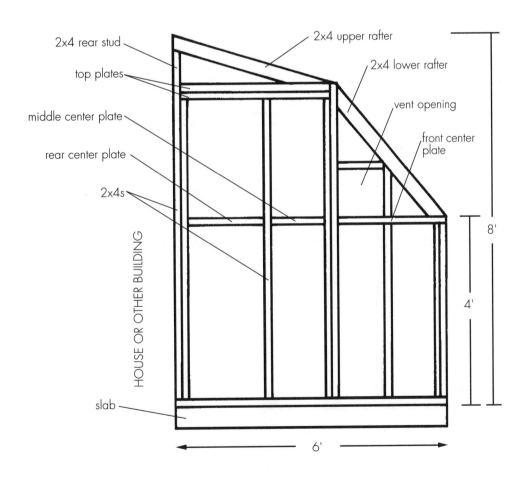

BACK ELEVATION

by truck to your house. These trucks can be extremely heavy, so make sure you have access to the pour from a driveway or street. Figure the amount of concrete needed according to the chart on page 8.

8. When the concrete is delivered you should have the tools needed to make the pour and finish the concrete ready and on hand. You can finish it yourself with a few hand tools, most of which can be obtained from a tool rental agency. You'll need a straight 2x4 that is 14 feet long, shovels for moving the concrete, and an old rake to help pull concrete around and to settle it in place. You'll also need some old rubber boots, a hand trowel, and a bull float.

9. Once the concrete has been poured into the form, rake it around and then jab the rake

head up and down over the surface to settle the concrete. You can wade through the wet concrete in the old boots as you work; it should be slightly higher than the form at this time.

10. Then with two people — one on each end — place the 14-foot 2x4 "screed" against the house foundation and "strike-off" the concrete by dragging the excess toward the front of the form. At the same time work the 2x4 back and forth in short movements to help settle the concrete in place and roughly smooth it up. Screeding is hard work but very necessary. You may have to make several passes to ensure the concrete is level with the form in all directions. If there are low spots, shovel concrete into them as you go and continue screeding until the material is level. The concrete surface can

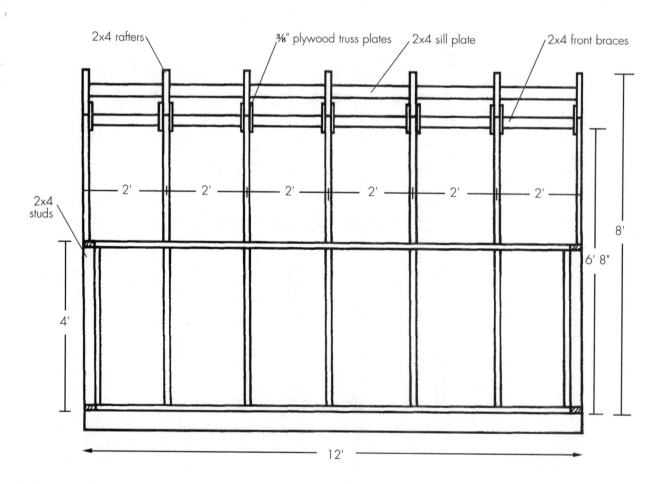

SIDE ELEVATION

114

be smoothed using the bull float, which is a large flat aluminum float with a long handle attached to it. Lift the float and place it on one end of the pour. Pull it slowly and evenly toward you to smooth the surface. At the end of the pull, drop the handle down and push it back or lift it and place it next to the end of the first pull. Repeat until the surface is smooth and uniform.

11. The wood framing for the greenhouse is held to the concrete pad with bolts set in the concrete while it is still wet. These are L-shaped special anchor bolts used just for the purpose. Measure along the form and make marks for each bolt location, normally placed in each corner and between every other stud. Make sure they won't protrude where a stud or upright is to be located. They should also be spaced approximately 1½ inches in from the inside edge of the form and should protrude approximately 2¼ inches above the wet concrete. Push the bolts down into the wet concrete and use the point of a trowel to smooth up the concrete around them. Allow the concrete to set up for 24 hours, then remove the form boards.

12. Begin framing the structure by creating the front end. Fasten the rear 2×4 stud to the house siding with 16d galvanized nails or counterbored lag screws.

13. Build the door header by nailing together the two 2×4s with a ⅜-inch spacer between them. Then cut the door support studs and toenail them to the underside of the header on each end. Stand the door frame assembly in position and nail the back door support stud to the rear stud.

14. Build the small front end section by cutting the center stud, the three short studs, and the bottom and center plates. Lay these pieces on the floor and nail the bottom plate to both the long center stud and the two short front studs. Then nail the center plate on top of the front studs and where it abuts the center stud. Nail the third short stud in the center between the center and bottom plates. Locate the anchor bolt holes in the bottom plate and

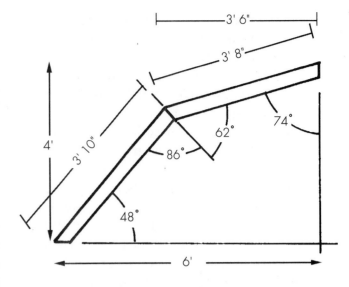

TRUSS RAFTERS

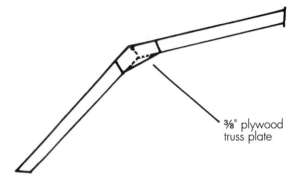

⅜" plywood truss plate

TRUSS PLATE

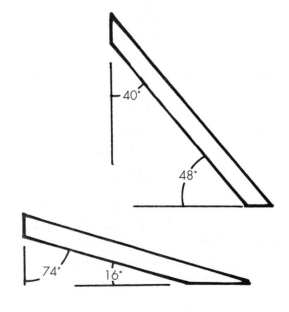

ANGLES FOR TRUSS RAFTERS

bore. Then lift this section up and position it down over the bolts; nail the center stud to the door stud.

15. Cut the lower rafter and nail it in place (see box on page 153). Then cut the upper rafter and toenail it into the house siding. Saw the vent opening pieces to fit between the lower rafter and center plate and center stud. A good way to get the proper angle is to cut the bottom of the vertical piece square, hold it against the rafter in the correct position, and mark the proper angle. Then cut the horizontal piece.

16. Construction of the back end is done in much the same manner. Again, anchor the rear stud to the house siding. Assemble the rear wall section. Bore the holes for the bolts, then stand this in place (slipping it down over the bolts), and fasten it to the stud. Assemble the front section, slip it down over the bolts, and fasten the front to the rear section.

17. Cut and fasten the rafters as before, then finish with the framing around the ventilator door. Cut the top plates that fit between the top ends of the upper rafters and nail them with 16d nails in position against the house siding. Then nail the upper ends of the top rafters into each end of the plates.

18. Assemble the lower side wall section on the concrete floor by cutting the lower and center plates to size, as well as the studs that fit between them. Fasten studs in position between plates with 16d galvanized nails. Measure and drill for the anchor bolts, and then raise the side assembly up and drop it into position. Anchor with nuts on the bolts and by nailing the outer studs into the end unit studs.

19. Cut the sill plate and nail it to the outside vertical studs. Then cut the front and back top rafters as shown in the drawing of truss rafters and nail them to the front wall and to the header on the back wall. Cut the bottom rafters and nail them on the front and back as well. The remaining interior rafters are actually trusses. Cut the upper and lower truss rafters to the angles shown, cut the truss plates, and fasten the trusses together. Install the trusses in position on the front plate and back wall sill plates. Place a truss on the inside of both the front and back walls at the rafter junction. Cut the 2x4 upper front braces to fit between the rafters and install by toenailing in place.

20. The entire greenhouse is covered with Filon greenhouse panels. Start applying on the ends. Install the wooden filler strips on the bottom plate and on the horizontals. Note that the strips won't work on the rafters due to the angle of the rafters. Leave the door and ventilator spaces open. Cut the panel sections to size and install, starting at the back of the greenhouse. Galvanized metal roofing nails with neoprene washers anchor the panels. Don't drive the nails too deeply or you may dent the panels. If you don't drive them deeply enough, however, they will leak at the nail holes. Continue installing until the back is covered. You may need to practice a bit.

21. Install the side wall paneling, starting at the side away from the prevailing wind. Then install the lower roof section, overlapping the side wall by about 2 inches. The roof section overlaps the end walls by about 1 inch. To waterproof and windproof the joints, use a clear caulking such as Magic Seal.

22. The ventilator doors can be made of plywood with hinges and simple hooks to hold them open, or you can utilize special solar vents that open and close within specific temperature ranges. If you choose the latter, buy them before beginning the project so you can customize their fit.

23. A wooden frame can be made and covered with the solar panels for the door, but the opening is a standard size, and the best tactic is to purchase a 36-inch-wide aluminum metal storm door which provides glass to see into your greenhouse and open screening for ventilation on hotter days. Since they are prehung, these door units are also easy to install.

GREENHOUSE BENCHES AND FLATS

IF YOU HAVE A GREENHOUSE, then you probably need benches or tables to hold planting trays, pots, and other greenhouse supplies. The benches shown are specifically designed to fit both the portable greenhouse and the add-on greenhouse described in this book. Bench #1 has top and lower shelves covered with hardware cloth to keep them open and let water drain through. Bench #2 has a wooden top on one end that can be used as a potting bench as well as a wood-covered shelf below to hold pots, potting soil, and other supplies. Naturally the materials used for these benches must be of a water-resistant and strong material such as pressure-treated wood.

Construction

Begin construction of Bench #1 by cutting the pieces for the ends and legs and joining the horizontal pieces to the legs using 16d galvanized nails. Make sure the end leg assemblies are square with a carpenter's square.

GREENHOUSE BENCH #1
MATERIALS LIST

- 6 Legs: 2 × 4 × 36"
- 4 End horizontals: 2 × 4 × 34"
- 2 Center dividers: 2 × 4 × 31"
- 4 Side horizontals: 2 × 4" × 11'3"
- 2 Hardware cloth sheets: 36" × 12'

GREENHOUSE BENCH #2
MATERIALS LIST

- 6 Legs: 2 × 4 × 36"
- 4 End horizontals: 2 × 4 × 34"
- 2 Center dividers: 2 × 4 × 31"
- 4 Side horizontals: 2 × 4" × 11'3"
- 2 Shelves:
  ⅝ treated plywood × 34 × 69½"
- 1 Top back edge: ¾ × 1½ × 69½"
- 2 Side edges: ¾ × 1½ × 33¼"
- 2 Hardware cloth sheets: 36" × 6'

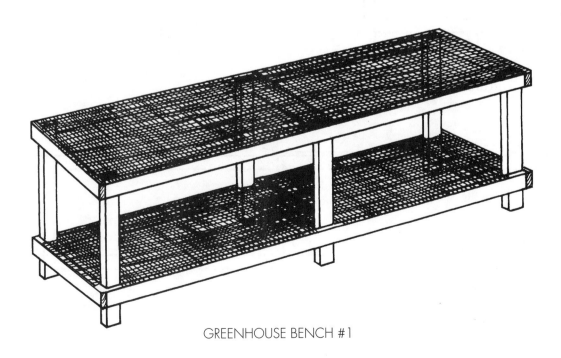

GREENHOUSE BENCH #1

Cut the side horizontal pieces, lay the end assemblies on their sides, and fasten the top and bottom horizontal pieces across both ends. Again, make sure the units are assembled squarely. Turn the unit over and nail on the opposite horizontal side pieces. Then stand the unit upright and cut and attach the two center dividers. Saw the center horizontal divider supports to length and nail them between the horizontal dividers and to the leg posts.

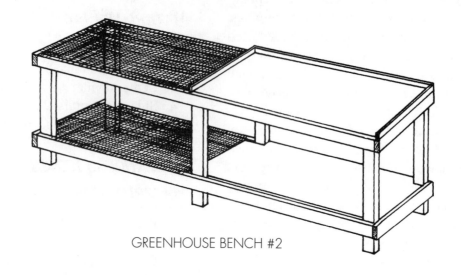

GREENHOUSE BENCH #2

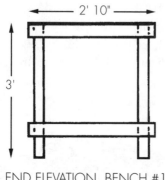

END ELEVATION, BENCH #1

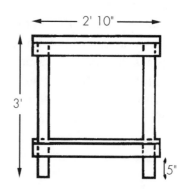

END ELEVATION, BENCH #2 WOOD SHELF END

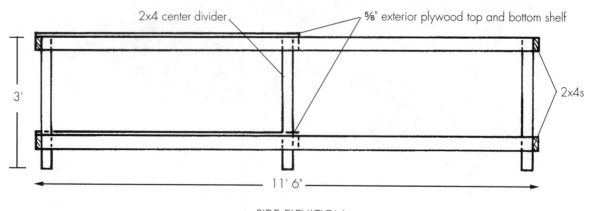

2x4 center divider

⅝" exterior plywood top and bottom shelf

3'

2x4s

11' 6"

SIDE ELEVATION

64 Yard & Garden Projects You Can Build Yourself

Trim one sheet of the hardware cloth to cover the bottom shelf, notching around the posts and fastening with galvanized staples. Make sure no sharp ends protrude that can catch clothing or cause scratches. Trim the top hardware cloth sheet to length and fasten in the same manner.

For Bench #2, assemble just like Bench #1 except for the solid wood end portion.

Then fasten the bottom shelf in place, notching around the legs and center dividers and fastening with 8d galvanized nails. Cut the top shelf to size and attach. Then cut the top back and side edge boards to size and shape; fasten around the sides and back edge of the top shelf. The edge boards prevent pots and debris from falling off.

PLANTING FLATS

I've used homemade planting flats for many years. We sided our office in solid western rough-sawn cedar, so I used the scraps as sides for these flats and other scrap material for the bottoms. I even used parts of paneling or hardboard for bottoms, but they eventually rotted out and had to be replaced. With pressure-treated wood, I can now make flats that will last indefinitely.

Building planting flats is a simple chore that takes only a few minutes. If you're making up several flats, it's a good idea to cut and assemble them in assembly-line fashion. In other words, cut all the bottoms, then all the long side pieces, and finally all the short end pieces for the number you intend to assemble.

Stack the pieces up on a flat work surface and begin nailing them together with 6d nails. Stand side pieces on the work surface; lay an end piece on top of them and fasten in place with 6d galvanized nails. Then turn the assembly over and nail the opposite end piece down on the two side pieces. Finally, lay the frame assembly flat, position the bottom in place, square up the assembly with a carpenter's square, and attach the bottom with 4d galvanized nails.

Incidentally, you don't need to build the flats the same size as shown here — you can fit them to

your own needs. You may want them square rather than rectangular or perhaps deeper.

To use the flats, I line the bottoms with newspaper and add a mixture of one part compost and one part milled sphagnum moss that has perlite or another moisture-holding material. The newspaper in the bottom helps retain moisture and also makes lifting out soil and plants easier.

PLANTING FLATS MATERIALS LIST

2 Ends: ¾ × 2 × 12"
2 Sides: ¾ × 2 × 16½"
1 Bottom: ¼ plywood × 12 × 18"

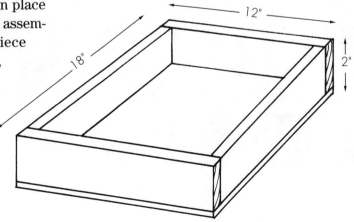

Projects for the Yard

AROUND-THE-TREE BENCH

A WOODEN BENCH SEAT constructed around a tree offers a comfortable and pleasant seating arrangement as well as a cool spot to relax in the shade during the summer heat. As a permanent part of your property, it can also add to the beauty, usefulness, and investment of your yard and home.

Naturally, for an around-the-tree bench the first step is to locate the right tree. In the case of the bench shown, the tree is located between a patio barbecue area and a vegetable garden. In the past we often pulled chairs under the tree to clean or prepare vegetables fresh from the garden and then moved the chairs over by the barbecue so guests could visit while cooking. Our big old oak is in the ideal location for sitting and provides lots of summer shade. Unfortunately, it is huge and has a distinct tilt to the south. Making sure the bench really will fit around your tree without crowding it or causing damage should be your first consideration. On smaller trees you can easily determine whether the bench will fit, and on some large trees merely holding a yardstick up against the tree and "eyeballing" the

A bench seat constructed around a tree can provide a comfortable, shady spot to relax or do garden chores.

approximate diameter will work. If there is still doubt, be certain to accurately determine the diameter first to ensure the bench will fit around the tree. Although not all trees are really circular, one way to estimate the tree's diameter is to measure its circumference and divide that figure by three. The diameter of a circle is a little more than one-third the length of the circumference.

We constructed the seat in two sections consisting of three "supports," which were each then joined with the seat boards and back. We then positioned these assemblies against the tree on some old lawn chairs and measured the two connecting seat sections.

This project is a good use of quality pressure-treated wood. Using any other type of untreated wood will decrease the life of the bench, and the splintering, twisting, warping, and cracking that will subsequently occur can make the seat uncomfortable and unsightly in a short amount of time. With pressure-treated wood your around-the-tree bench should last a lifetime.

As for tools, you could conceivably build the project with hand tools alone, but a portable circular saw, power drill, and power wrench can speed the process. A radial arm or table saw will also make the job much easier and faster, especially when making repetitive angled cuts, and can help the fitting process be more precise.

In a sense, this project is a fooler; it looks deceptively easy, but the number of angles and the relatively complicated construction techniques take a bit of figuring, patience, and woodworking skill. The average woodworker, however, with some shop skills and power tools should be able to build the bench quite easily in a couple of weekends.

Seat support assemblies are constructed first. Nail them together with galvanized nails. You can strengthen the seat further by boring holes through the assembly ends and installing bolts.

AROUND-THE-TREE BENCH MATERIALS LIST

6	Seat boards: 2 × 4 × 40½" **(A)**
6	Seat boards: 2 × 4 × 36" **(B)**
6	Seat boards: 2 × 4 × 31½" **(C)**
6	Seat boards: 2 × 4 × 27" **(D)**
12	Outer back supports: 2 × 4 × 11" **(E)**
6	Center back supports: 2 × 4 × 15" **(F)**
6	Seat support dividers: 2 × 4 × 5¼" **(G)**
12	Outside seat supports: 2 × 4 × 21" **(H)**
6	Back boards: 2 × 4 × 20" **(I)**
6	Back boards: 2 × 4 × 21½" **(J)**
6	Back boards: 2 × 4 × 23" **(K)**
6	Posts: 4 × 4 × 36" **(L)**

Use only quality pressure-treated lumber and galvanized nails for constructing the bench.

Fasten three seat support assemblies together to make two seat sections.

Prop the assemblies around the tree to check that they are properly positioned.

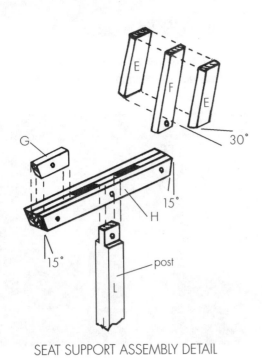

SEAT SUPPORT ASSEMBLY DETAIL

Construction

1. Begin by cutting all the angled seat and back boards. Regardless of whether you are using power or hand tools, I suggest that you set up and cut all similar pieces at the same time to ensure that all angles are precisely cut to match. For instance, make all 30-degree cuts at one time. If you are using a handsaw or portable circular saw, use a protractor and bevel gauge to mark the angles. If using a stationary power saw, set the tool to 30 degrees and cut all like pieces at once. Then cut all the 15-degree pieces and, finally, all the 10-degree pieces.

Note that the outer back supports (E) are beveled 30 degrees ½ inch back on their front edges. It's a good idea to bevel the stock before cutting the pieces to length.

2. When all pieces are the correct length, lay an outside seat support piece (H) on a sturdy work surface. Lay a center back support piece (F) and a seat support divider piece (G) on top of this and fasten in place with galvanized 8d nails. Note that these nails must be placed around the outside edges, as the center will have a bolt hole drilled through it. Position another outside seat support piece (H) over the top of the assembly and nail it down. Nail the outer back support pieces (E) in place and then measure and bore the bolt holes through both ends as well as the center for the support post (L). Install the bolts in both the front and back of the supports.

3. Cut the posts to the proper length and then lay out the tenons which fit into the seat supports (see drawing at left). This can be done with hand tools by using a square to mark off each tenon. To cut, first saw across the stock down to the depth of the tenon on both sides. Repeat this process on both sides to create the tenon. If using a radial arm or table saw, set the saw to the correct depth and use continuous cuts to remove the material on both sides of the tenon. A dado blade that can be adjusted to make wider cuts can be used to speed the pro-

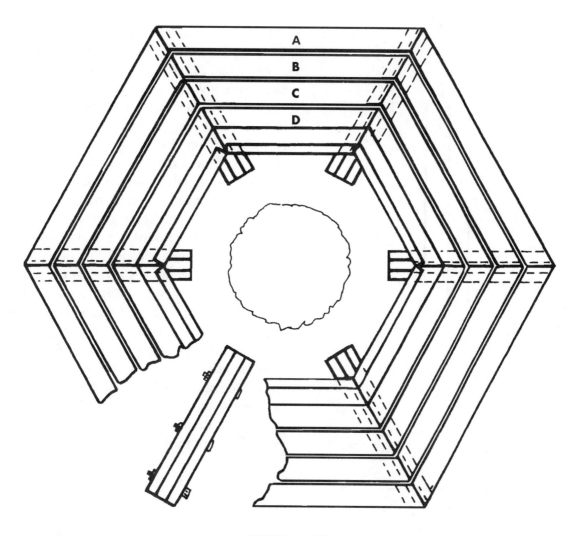

OVERHEAD VIEW

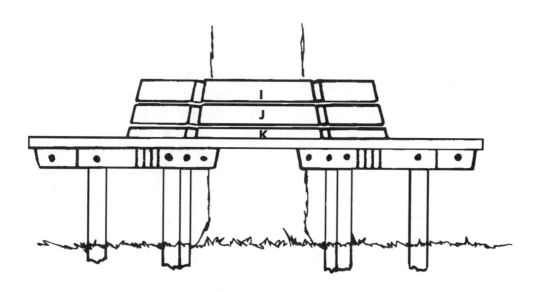

SIDE ELEVATION

PROJECTS FOR THE YARD

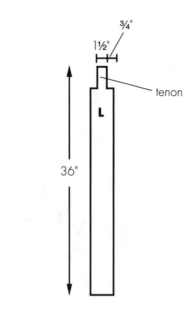

LAYOUT OF TENON ON POST

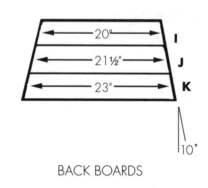

BACK BOARDS

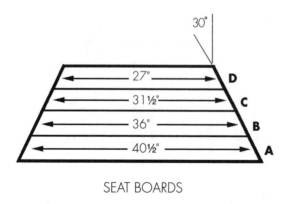

SEAT BOARDS

cess. However, as pressure-treated lumber is fairly hard, don't cut with the blade wider than ⅜ inch. Test-fit each post into the support to make sure it will fit properly.

4. The next step is to assemble two seats on top of three supports to make up two sections. Position the supports on a smooth surface such as a garage or shop floor and begin by temporarily nailing with 8d nails the lowest back crosspieces (K) in place from the center support to each side support. Then tack-nail the back seat board (D). Make sure each end meets the center of each support and that each support assembly is sitting at the proper angle, which you can confirm by measuring from the sides of the support edges and adjusting the position and angle of the supports as needed. Tack-nail the remainder of the seat boards until you are sure the supports are at the correct angle and the seat boards all meet properly. Once the entire assembly is properly assembled, drive the nails down securely. Because many of these nails will be close to the ends of the stock, it's a good idea to predrill holes for the nails in the seat boards to prevent splitting the stock; use a drill bit slightly smaller than the size of the nail. Once all seat boards have been installed on a support assembly, the remainder of the back boards are nailed in place as well.

5. When you have an entire support section assembled, turn it upside down and install the post by boring a hole through the hole in the support into the post tenon; bolt it in place. As the posts have a tendency to move back and forth somewhat at this time, it's also a good idea to drive a couple of 16d galvanized nails through the bottom supports and into the posts to keep them firmly positioned until the entire unit can be solidly anchored in the ground. You can also ensure at this time that the posts won't sink in the future by driving large nails about half of their length approximately 2 inches up from the bottoms of the posts. When the nails set in the concrete, the posts are locked in the ground.

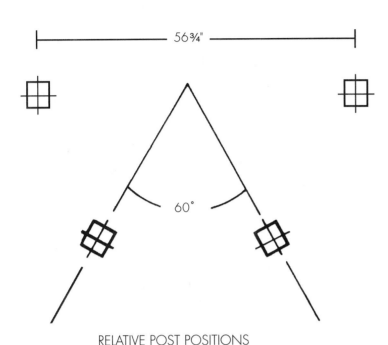

RELATIVE POST POSITIONS

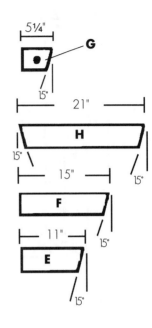

PIECES CUT WITH 15° ANGLES

6. Since each three-post section must be anchored in the ground at the proper distance from the tree as well as the correct length and angle from each other, the additional sections can be installed. The section posts must be placed in the ground with concrete poured around them. A distinct problem is the possibility of placing posts directly over tree roots. In fact, you might as well count on it. Cutting through or around a root is not only a headache to you, but a "rootache" to the tree; it could even kill it.

7. There are several solutions to this problem. The first is to position the sections and posts around the tree and to measure to ensure everything properly meets. Shift the sections around the tree so the posts miss any obvious roots. Mark the locations of the holes and dig exploratory holes. If any holes meet major roots, shift the sections and try again. I told you this wasn't an easy project, but the results are worth it. If you meet a root that can't be avoided, then that post will have to be shortened appropriately. If you are simply stymied by roots, a second possibility is to cut the posts to ground level and sink half-sized concrete blocks in place and set the entire assembly on this. Since the blocks won't be cemented down, the bench won't be nearly as solid. Unfortunately, you may not have a choice.

8. If you're able to place the posts in holes, dig the holes to the proper depth and position the sections with the posts down in the holes (see drawing). Use a level to make sure each section is level and that it matches the other posts. Finding the right position will take some digging and reshuffling, so it's a good idea to have a helper or two on hand. Gravel placed in the bottom of the holes provides drainage and can be added or removed as needed to level the posts correctly.

9. Once you've got each section in the proper position, tack-nail the bottom back

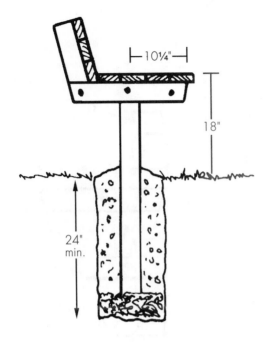

$\vdash 10\frac{1}{4}" \dashv$

18"

24" min.

SETTING POSTS IN HOLES WITH CONCRETE

Finally, fasten posts to each section. Dig holes for the posts, position the sections in place, and fasten them together with the remaining seat boards and back rests.

pieces to join the two sections together. Check again to make sure all sections are level, then tack-nail the remaining seat boards of the two joining sections to the completed sections. Once you're sure everything is level and fits properly, hammer the final nails to the seat boards.

10. Mix your concrete and pour it around the posts, making sure to tamp the concrete solidly down around the posts to settle it around the nails in the posts. The concrete should be mounded up slightly above ground level and smoothed down to force water to drain away from the posts. Allow the concrete to cure solidly before nailing the remaining back support pieces in place.

11. One other problem can occur. The area under the bench will have to be weeded by hand or by a weed trimmer. One solution is to place a plastic border guard around the outside circumference of the posts (if the tree roots don't interfere) and then fill the area below the posts with decorative mulch such as rocks or bark. The outside of the circumference can then be leveled with topsoil and reseeded to suit. Of course, this work will have to be done before the concrete is poured to set the posts. Another alternative is to place the border guard in a circle approximately 2½ feet away from the outside edge of the posts and to fill the entire area with mulch, decorative rocks, or even bricks on sand. Bricks make an attractive sidewalk-like area around the bench.

12. Although treated lumber will weather to a beautiful gray, I suggest you apply a coat of protective preservative designed for pressure-treated wood or, if you prefer, paint or stain it to suit your existing color scheme. Then it's time to sit back and enjoy your new bench.

COMPOST BIN

CLEANING UP your yard and garden in the fall from a season of gardening, grass cutting, leaf collection, and fallen tree debris is important for several reasons. A little work each fall will cut down on a great deal of work the following spring. Your yard, garden, and home in general will look neater through the winter months and, most important, these chores will help you maintain your investment in your property. Composting makes this work easier. In addition, composting helps solve the problem of overflowing city landfills while providing your garden with high-quality soil for bigger and healthier vegetables, flowers, and shrubs. Perhaps best of all, recycling your garden and yard debris is easier and less costly than bagging and carrying trash to the curb for pickup.

You can, of course, compost by simply piling recyclable debris in an out-of-the-way place, but compost is more easily made in a bin that holds the materials together while allowing air to penetrate. Compost bin designs vary a great deal from a simple wire cage to an expensive plastic or wood bin.

Actually, two or three compost bins are better to have than one. You can then "turn" one compost pile by pitching it into a second, start a new batch in the first, and then pitch the second bin as it "finishes" into a third. Thus, you can keep compost working at all times.

This wooden compost bin is made of treated lumber, with the front pieces simply stacked in place in the side slots. You can easily add or remove materials from the bin by removing the front slats.

MAKING A WIRE COMPOST CAGE

You can quickly make a simple compost cage with a 4-foot-high wall of welded reinforcing mesh wire. Form cages with a 6-foot circumference and join the ends by crimping. However, wire will eventually rust through and is not as sturdy as a wooden bin.

COMPOST BIN MATERIALS LIST

12	Side slats: 1 x 6 x 36"
6	Back slats: 1 x 6 x 45"
6	Front slats: 1 x 6 x 44½"
2	Back vertical supports: 2 x 2 x 36"
2	Front vertical supports: 2 x 2 x 36"
2	Front inside cleats: 2 x 2 x 36"
1	Bottom front cleat: 1 x 2 x 46½"
1	Top spreader cleat: 1 x 2 x 52½"
2	Top spread cleat ends: 1 x 2 x 3"

Construction

Start by cutting all side, back, and front slat pieces to the correct length from 1×6 pressure-treated lumber. The back and front vertical supports come from 2×4 stock. Rip a 2×4 to create two 2×2s (actually 1½ inches by 1½ inches) for the front inside cleats as well, which hold the slats.

Lay the back and front vertical supports for one side, plus one front inside cleat, on a smooth surface. Nail side slats down over them with the back vertical ¾ inch in from the slat edges, and the slats spaced out to fit verticals, allowing about ½ inch between boards. Build the opposite side in the same manner.

With the two sides completed, stand them on edge and position a back slat across the bottom between the two sides. Nail to the back verticals. Continue nailing the back slats in place. Cut the bottom front holding cleat and nail it in place over the front of the 2×2s and side slats.

Position the bin in place, drop the front slats into place between the front verticals and the front cleats. Create the top spreader cleat, which is simply a 1×2 with cleat ends nailed on each end. When placed over the top front edge of the bin it prevents the sides from spreading out.

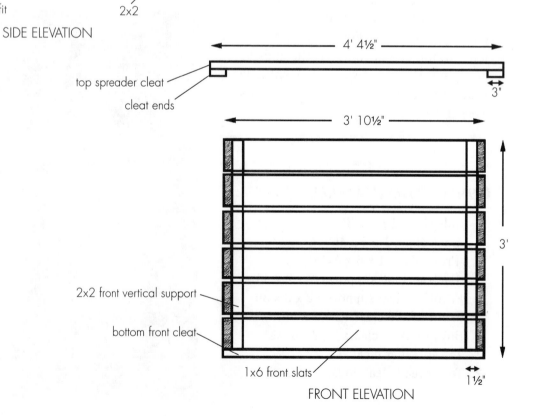

3'

3'

1×6s spaced to fit   2×2

SIDE ELEVATION

4' 4½"

top spreader cleat
cleat ends

3"

3' 10½"

3'

2×2 front vertical support

bottom front cleat

1×6 front slats

1½"

FRONT ELEVATION

COMPOSTING

Composting is easy with the proper tools. Although not a necessity, a chipper-shredder is one tool that can really help. A pile of leaves and other bulky garden debris will eventually break down into compost, but chopping materials into smaller pieces makes composting faster and takes up less space in the compost pile.

As you clean your yard and garden of debris, place the materials in separate piles near the place you will compost them. Throughout the spring and summer, use a grass bag on your lawn mower and pile the clippings near the compost area. Add weeds, vegetable tops, and other plant remains. This process makes your garden and yard look neater, removes weed seeds and insect pests from the garden, and results in easier gardening next spring. Properly done, composting kills most weed seeds and insect pests harbored in the vegetation.

In the fall, prune back all shrubs and trees after your plants have lost their leaves. The medium-sized and small limbs as well as twigs and vegetable stalks will need to be run through a chipper-shredder for more efficient decomposition. Clean up all fallen and rotted fruits or vegetables to prevent any continuation of pest problems.

Rake or gather fallen leaves with a yard vacuum, blower, or a mulcher-vacuum attachment on your lawn mower. Clean the leaves from your gutter using a vacuum or leaf blower. Pile the leaves near the compost area and cover them with plastic or tarps if you can't get the leaves into the compost bins immediately.

Once you have your yard and garden cleaned and the materials gathered near the composting area, simply add them to the compost bin in layers. Start with a layer of loose materials on the bottom, such as whole leaves and small branches, to provide aeration. Then create alternate layers, switching between lighter materials such as leaves and twigs and denser, heavier materials such as grass clippings. The pile should be 3 to 4 feet high for best results. Rotted manure, sweet clover, sewage sludge, natural fertilizers, and kitchen scraps can also be added to help introduce nitrogen to the pile and to speed the decomposition of the materials. The best tactic is to layer leaves or grass clippings with high-nitrogen materials, followed by a little topsoil. Once the pile is 3 to 4 feet high, cover with a tarp or a piece of black plastic mulch held down with branches, pieces of wood, rocks, or stakes.

Place a thermometer into the side of the pile and wait a couple of weeks, until the pile temperature has reached 110 to 120 degrees Fahrenheit and starts dropping. This is the best time to turn the pile. After this point turn the pile about every three days. Watch the temperature. It should reach 140 to 160 degrees to kill insect pests and weed seeds. After about four weeks the pile should not heat up after it has been turned; the composting process is finished. Two compost bins make the chore easier as you can move the material into the second from the first and then start the first one again, or move one batch of compost back and forth between the two as you turn it.

The valuable compost you've created can then be used to better your garden by simply digging it into your soil. If the compost reached between 140 and 160 degrees, it's fairly well sterilized; you can even bag some of it for potting soil for next spring. Compost is also great to use around trees and shrubs when setting them out, for digging in rhubarb or asparagus, and many other garden chores.

For more detailed information on making and using composting, refer to Stu Campbell's *Let It Rot!* from Garden Way Publishing.

GARDEN CART

THE WOODSHED is some distance from our house and through the winter months we have to haul a lot of wood to feed our 4-foot-wide fireplace. I quickly discovered that when it comes to carrying heavy loads — like four or five big logs — over rough and uneven ground a wheelbarrow is worse than useless. Add an inch or two of snow and you can forget about even trying to use the wheelbarrow. We also wanted something we could use to haul straw and hay bales to mulch our garden as well as carry rocks for my ongoing building projects around the house.

My solution is a heavy-duty garden cart made entirely of pressure-treated wood for durability and strength. The sides, bottom, and front and back end pieces are all cut from ⅜-inch treated plywood, and the cart is designed so all these pieces can be cut from one 4×8 sheet if you lay them out carefully before cutting. The wheels are sturdy solid rubber because we have thorn trees and bramble bushes scattered over our farm and tube tires just don't hold up. The axle is a simple threaded rod.

Construction

Start by constructing the handles, which also serve as the underframe support. Cut them to length, then mark around their sides 8 inches from the end using a small square. Set a combination square to 1 inch and scribe a line from the end of the piece to the marked lines on their faces. Scribe a curved line at these joints to create a gentle curved cut. In order to cut rounded handle ends on the boards, clamp one of the handles in a solid wood vise and scribe lines ½ inch from all sides as a guide to round the edges. Cut to the lines with a heavy-duty wood rasp (a common half-round rasp would be fine) and smooth with progressively finer

GARDEN CART MATERIALS LIST

2 Handle/frame pieces: 2 × 4 × 72"
1 Bottom: ⅜ plywood × 30 × 48"
1 Back bottom support: 2 × 4 × 27"
1 Front bottom support: 2 × 4 × 27"
1 Center bottom support: 2 × 4 × 27"
2 Inner wheel supports: 2 × 4 × 11½"
2 Outer wheel supports: 2 × 6 × 8"
2 Sides: ⅜ plywood × 18 × 48"
1 Front: ⅜ plywood × 14 × 29½"
1 Back: ⅜ plywood × 14 × 29½"
8 Vertical cleats: ¾ × 1¼ × 14"
2 Horizonal side cleats: ¾ × 1¼ × 44"
2 Back legs: 2 × 4 × 19½"
2 Wheels: 20" bicycle type
1 Axle: ½" threaded rod, 40" long
6 Washers
6 Nuts

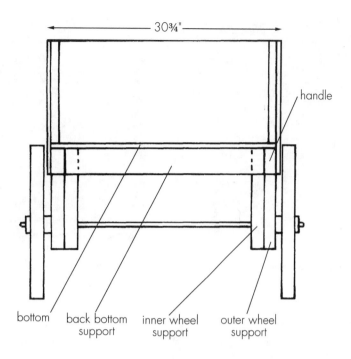

30¾"

handle

bottom   back bottom   inner wheel   outer wheel
support   support   support

REAR ELEVATION

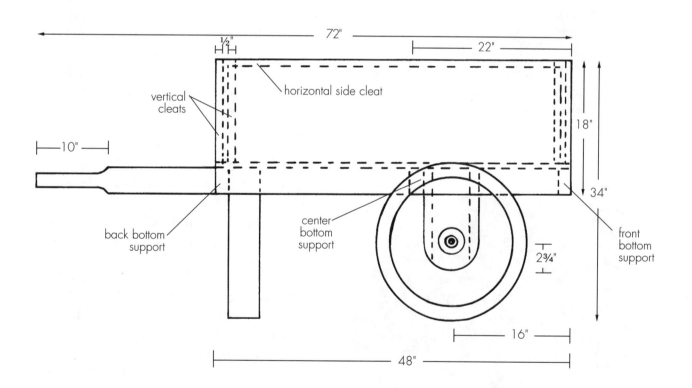

72"

½"

22"

horizontal side cleat

vertical
cleats

18"

10"

back bottom
support

center
bottom
support

2¾"

front
bottom
support

34"

16"

48"

SIDE ELEVATION

A drawknife makes shaping the handles much easier.

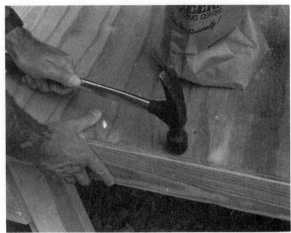

All plywood pieces should fit snugly and be free of splinters.

Turn the assembly upside down to fasten the legs in place.

Rip the cleats carefully using a ripping guide.

grits of sandpaper until you reach the lines and the handles are rounded and smooth. An alternative and much quicker method is to use a drawknife to shear the stock quickly and easily without necessitating a lot of extra sanding.

With the handle/frame pieces cut and smooth, lay them edge up on a flat surface. Cut the bottom piece from treated plywood, using a pair of sawhorses to hold the plywood sheet securely and making sure your portable circular saw's cuts are square and smooth. Lightly sand the edges to remove splinters; lay the cut bottom on the upper edges of the handle pieces and fasten firmly in place using 8d galvanized nails. The end of the bottom piece must be even with the front ends of the handle/frame pieces and the side edges must be flush with the outside edges.

Cut the front and back bottom support pieces from a 2×4, measuring to fit between the side handle pieces, and attach them between the side handle/frames using 16d galvanized nails hammered through the side pieces into the support pieces and 8d galvanized nails driven through the cart bottom into the support pieces.

Now turn this assembly upside down on a smooth, sturdy surface such as a pair of sawhorses or a workbench. Cut the back legs to length and fasten them inside the frame. Form the outer wheel support pieces from 2×6s by first cutting them to length and then rounding their ends using a band saw or saber saw with a heavy-duty blade (see drawing of side elevation). Cut the inner wheel support pieces from a 2x4 and round their ends as well. Fasten the two pieces together for each inner wheel support assembly using 16d nails or #10 2½-inch screws. Mark the locations for the axle and bore the axle holes making sure they are bored straight and in the proper position. Fasten these pieces in place with four #10 2½-inch screws driven through the outside of the handle/frame pieces into the wheel support pieces. Make sure the wheel supports are square with the assembly with a carpenter's square before fastening in place. A pair of large C-clamps can be used to hold the pieces firmly in place until you get them anchored properly.

Measure between the two side handle pieces for the center bottom support piece before cutting it to ensure you get a snug and proper fit. Fasten the support piece between the side handle pieces and against the back side of the wheel support pieces and anchor firmly in place with galvanized nails or screws.

Turn the assembly upright so that it rests on a pair of sawhorses to make up the "box" sides. Cut the sides from treated plywood, again making absolutely sure you have cut them squarely. Sand all edges lightly to remove any splinters.

The front and back pieces are removable so you can load from either end. They fit in grooves created by cleats fastened to the inside front and back edges of the sides. Cut these vertical and horizontal cleats first by ripping treated 1x6 stock to size using a stationary saw or a portable electric saw and ripping guide, and then crosscutting to length. Note that the vertical cleats are shorter than the height of the side pieces, because they fit above the bottom and the handle support pieces.

To assemble, place two vertical cleats on a flat surface; place one side piece on top of them, positioning the cleats at the outer edges of the side. Fasten the side down using

Rest the cart on sawhorses as you assemble the "box."

The front and back pieces slide into grooves formed by cleats.

Test for the right degree of snugness so the wheels turn freely before tightening the wheel-holding nuts completely.

4d galvanized nails. The two inside vertical cleats are spaced in from the outside cleats the width of the plywood plus ⅛ inch for clearance (to allow the pieces to slide up and down freely and evenly) and fastened in the same manner. Install one horizontal side cleat on the top edge of each side between the front and back cleats to strengthen the side.

Once these side assemblies have been constructed, install them with the cleat ends down against the cart bottom and the sides flush with the bottom edges of the handle pieces. Anchor with 4d galvanized nails. Use 8d galvanized nails at each crossmember location (front, back, and center).

Cut the front and back pieces to size and shape and sand their edges to remove any splinters. Slide them in place to try the fit.

To install the wheels turn the cart with the bottom side up on a pair of sawhorses. You might also require another pair of hands for this. Place two nuts and a washer and then a wheel over the threaded axle rod. Add another washer, then push the rod through the axle hole into one wheel support. Once the rod protrudes, thread on another washer and finally another nut. Continue threading the assembly through until you almost reach the hole in the opposite wheel support. Then put on another nut, add another washer, and complete threading the axle rod in place until the first wheel is in position against the wheel support. Tighten the interior nut snugly against the wheel sup-

port. Then place a washer over the threaded axle rod protruding from the opposite side, thread the wheel in place, and add another washer and the two outside nuts. Turn the inside nut up against the wheel support and then the two outside nuts until they are snug as well.

You'll have to experiment to get the wheel-holding nuts the correct snugness. You want the nuts tight enough to hold the wheels firmly in place but still allow the wheels to turn freely. Threaded rod is normally sold in 3-, 4-, and 6-foot lengths. You'll have to purchase a 4- or 6-foot length as 3 feet isn't long enough to extend the width of the cart. Once the rod is threaded in place, all wheels are installed, and the outside nuts have been snugged down, use a hacksaw to cut off the excess rod from one side.

Although the sides support themselves pretty well without splaying outward, you might wish to add screw-eyes to the sides and front and back pieces to keep them tight when transporting heavy materials such as compost, soil, or rocks. I estimate that the cart will carry 200–300 hundred pounds comfortably.

Make sure all edges and surfaces are sanded smooth and then finish to suit. The treated lumber doesn't actually require any type of finishing and will gradually weather to a beautiful gray. However, you may wish to provide additional protection by coating with a protective oil or a good quality gloss exterior enamel paint.

MOVABLE WORK CENTER

HAVE YOU EVER CARRIED a handful of rakes, hoes, and shovels to a flower bed, then returned to your garden shed for the potted plants and fertilizer, and then returned yet again for the garden trowel you forgot? If

MOVABLE WORK CENTER MATERIALS LIST

2   Front legs: 1½ × 1½ × 28"
2   Back legs: 1½ × 1½ × 30"
6   Side horizontals: 1½ × 1½ × 15½"
6   Front and back horizontals: 1½ × 1½ × 32"
2   Sides: ½ plywood × 18½ × 24"
1   Back: ½ plywood × 24 × 36"
2   Front side trims: ⅜ plywood × 2 × 22¼"
2   Doors: ½ plywood × 16 × 22¼"
1   Top: ½ plywood × 19½ × 36"
1   Shelf: ¾ plywood × 18½ × 35", cut to fit
1   Bottom: ½ plywood × 18½ × 35", cut to fit
1   Top side trim: ¾ × 1¾ × 18½"
2   Top front and back trims: ¾ × 1¾ × 48"
1   Handle: ¾ × 1¾ × 19½"
1   Top tool rack: ¾ × 3 × 19½"
1   Lower bottom tool rack: ¾ × 3 × 19½"
1   Upper bottom tool rack: ¾ × 3 × 19½"
1   Bottom tool rack support: ¾ × 3 × 19½"
1   Axle: ½" × 3' threaded rod
2   Wheels: 6" diameter, lawnmower type
2   Hinges: 2" butt
2   Pair magnetic door catch pairs
2   Door pulls

you're tired of all those trips, the movable work center is a project you'll appreciate. It's also useful for storing those items you use frequently in a convenient one-spot storage unit in your garage, keeping a good deal of the clutter off your floor, and preventing those rakes and hoes from falling off the wall hooks only to be stepped on or run over by your car. I know from experience what a hoe can do to a tire!

The unit shown is actually a small cabinet on wheels. There are two shelves inside, a work surface on top, and a rack to hold lawn and garden tools on the side. With purchased metal wheels placed on a threaded steel rod, the movable work center can easily be rolled to the work site with everything you need — including workspace for repotting — to work on your plants.

Construction

The cart is made of pressure-treated plywood and lumber. Start by cutting the back and side plywood pieces to the correct size. Note that all the pieces for this project can come from one sheet of plywood if you lay them out carefully.

Once the plywood pieces are cut, rip 2×4s for the legs and interior framing with a table or radial arm saw or with a rip fence on a portable electric saw. Crosscut the leg pieces to the correct length. Bore holes in the front legs for the wheels. Lay a front and rear leg on a flat work surface and nail the back piece to the legs using 4d galvanized nails.

Fasten the other front leg to one plywood side piece, then nail the side piece to the assembled back section with 6d or 8d nails. Next, attach a rear leg to the opposite side piece and nail the other end of the side piece to the assembled unit. Cut the side horizontal pieces to proper length by measuring between the legs and then cutting to fit. Saw the front and back horizontals and fasten them between the front legs with 8d galvanized nails.

Make notches in the bottom shelf to fit around the legs, position it in the cabinet, and fasten it with 4d galvanized nails. The upper shelf, however, won't fit if it is cut whole from the plywood. Instead, cut it from pieces of 1× material, slide them into place from the front, and anchor with 4d galvanized nails. Finally, cut the top piece to the correct size and nail it down on the side horizontals and leg posts using 4d galvanized nails.

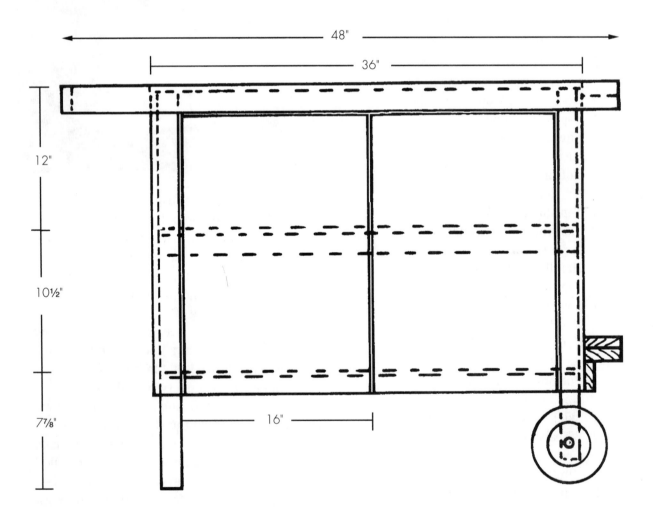

Rip the front, back, and side trim pieces from solid 1× stock and nail them to the top with 4d galvanized nails. Note that the side trim extends over the sides to provide an anchoring position for the handle and the tool rack. Once the front and back pieces are installed, saw the side trim pieces to fit and anchor in place. Saw the handle to size, fasten it in place between the front and back trim pieces with #10 2-inch screws driven through the trim into the handle ends. Once you've cut the top tool rack to size, you will need to think about what tools you want it to hold. Bore holes sized for your particular tools using a hole cutter and a portable electric drill. Incidentally, this task is made a heck of a lot easier with a drill press if you have access to one. With the top tool rack as a template, bore matching holes in the upper bottom tool rack. Fasten the top rack piece between the front and back trim pieces with screws.

Assemble the bottom rack by fastening the upper and lower bottom rack pieces — and then the bottom tool rack support piece — with screws. Finally, anchor the completed bottom rack to the assembly with wood screws driven through the bottom rack into the bottom end of the unit.

Cut the door and the front side trim strips to size and lock trim in place with 4d galvanized nails. Install the two doors with butt hinges fastened to the doors and trim pieces. The doors are held shut with simple magnetic door catches. If you wish you can make the unit even more decorative by adding vertical corner trim and painting it in a color that contrasts with the plywood sides. If you cover the top of the unit with plastic laminate (like Formica), you will have a waterproof, smooth, and easily cleaned surface that can double as an outside working surface for cleaning produce.

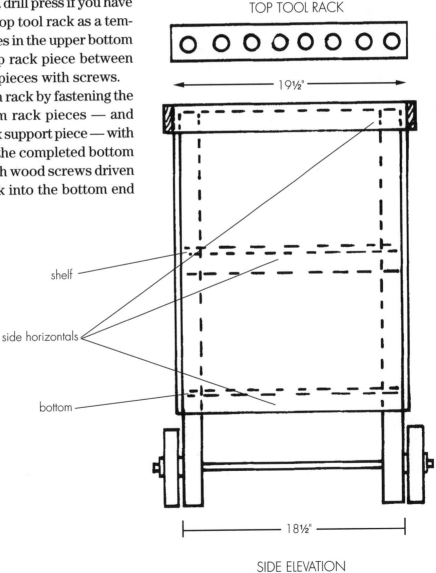

TOP TOOL RACK

19½"

shelf

side horizontals

bottom

18½"

SIDE ELEVATION

POTTING TABLE AND SOIL BIN

POTTING TABLE MATERIALS LIST

4 Legs: 2 × 4 × 36"
4 Front and back crosspieces:
    2 × 4 × 48"
4 Upper and lower end crosspieces:
    2 × 4 × 24"
5 Bottom shelf boards: 1 × 6 × 48"
5 Top boards: 1 × 6 × 48"
1 Back skirt board: 1 × 6 × 48"
2 End skirt boards: 1 × 6 × 27¾"

ALTHOUGH LABELED a "potting" table, this sturdy workbench is invaluable for potting, transplanting, and labeling plants — as well as many other garden chores. It can be made of pressure-treated materials or untreated woods like redwood or western white cedar, depending on your preference. With weather-resistant building supplies, the table can be left outside, near the garden, under a carport, or in a back corner of your yard. If made of untreated wood, sanded smooth, and topped with a coat of varnish, the table will look nice in a corner of your patio, greenhouse, or garden shed.

I designed the table to be 36 inches high, which is just about perfect for a person of average height to work comfortably while standing. You may, however, wish to change the height to suit your individual stature. The back and sides of the top have a skirt around the edges to keep pots and other items from sliding off. The table also has a bottom shelf that can be used to hold pots, soil in tubs or buckets, or anything else you can think of.

Construction

First, saw the legs from 2×4 stock, then cut the upper and lower end crosspieces to the proper length. Fasten the crosspieces to the legs using 16d galvanized nails. Make sure the crosspieces are nailed level across the legs to create a rigidly rectangular frame. A carpenter's square is a good tool for checking your measurements.

Cut the front and back crosspieces to length, stand two end leg frames on their sides, and fasten an upper and lower front crosspiece in place with 16d galvanized nails. Then, turn the assembly over and fasten the back upper and lower crosspieces. Again, make absolutely sure the frame is square with a carpenter's square or by measuring the diagonals.

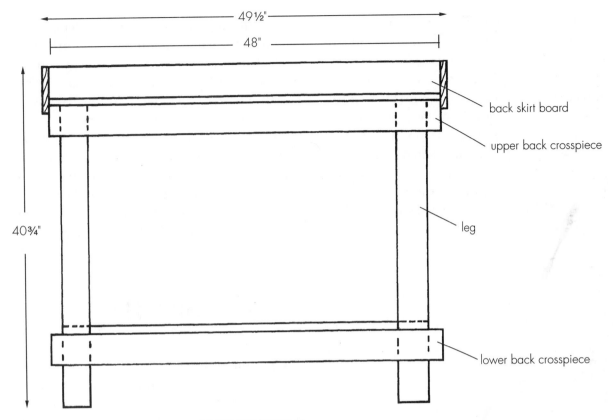

49½"

48"

40¾"

back skirt board

upper back crosspiece

leg

lower back crosspiece

BACK ELEVATION

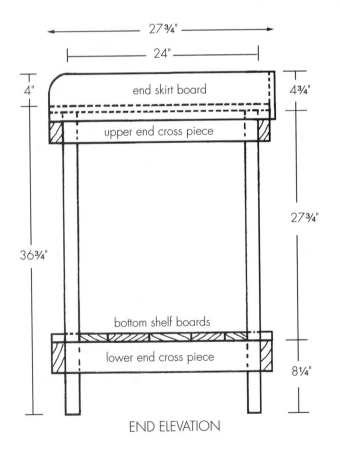

27¾"

24"

4"

4¾"

end skirt board

upper end cross piece

27¾"

36¾"

bottom shelf boards

lower end cross piece

8¼"

END ELEVATION

139

Measure and saw the bottom 1×6 shelf boards to length. Note that you will have to form notches for the legs on the front and back and the back shelf board must be ripped to the correct width. Cut the notches first with a portable electric saw and finish with a handsaw or saber saw. Rip the back board to the correct width using a ripping guide and portable electric circular saw or a radial arm or table saw. Fasten the bottom shelf boards on the bottom support frame using 8d galvanized nails.

Cut the top boards to the correct length and fasten them on the top framework with 8d galvanized nails as well. Cut the back skirt board to the proper length and nail it in place using 8d galvanized nails hammered through the skirt board into the back top framework.

When you have cut the two end skirt boards to length, mark the circumference of the rounded front end on each board. These can be cut with a saber saw or band saw. Anchor the skirt boards to the end frames and the back skirt board with 8d galvanized nails.

POTTING SOIL BIN

The potting soil bin pictured with the potting table is easy to create from ⅜-inch pressure-treated plywood. You may want to make two or three to hold different materials such as peat and compost.

Construction

Cut the two sides to size before making their angled front edges (see drawing). Shape the front and back pieces and carefully nail them to the sides with 4d galvanized nails. Cut the bottom, turn the assembly upside down, and nail it in place.

POTTING SOIL BIN MATERIALS LIST

2 Sides: ⅜ plywood × 18 × 22"
1 Back: ⅜ plywood × 18 × 18"
1 Front: ⅜ plywood × 12 × 18"
1 Bottom: ⅜ plywood × 18 × 22"

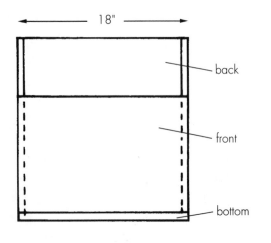

FRONT ELEVATION

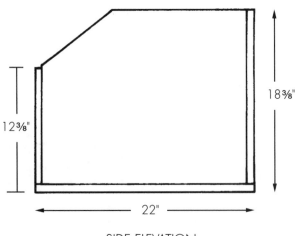

SIDE ELEVATION

PORTABLE GARDEN SHED

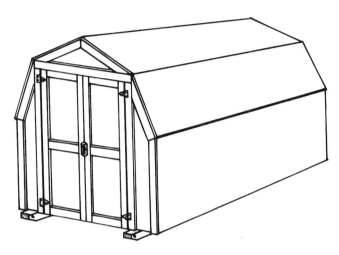

GARDEN SHEDS are often very practical additions to homes in the suburbs and countryside. Sheds can be used to store garden tractors, lawn mowers, tillers, rakes, hoes, and all your other garden and lawn tools. Sheds should at least blend in with the existing architecture, but they can be a focal point of a backyard or garden setting. This shed has a gambrel roof, which makes the shed more attractive and provides more headroom. Although this gambrel design appears somewhat complicated, it's really an easy project, even for the first-timer.

Since it is constructed on skids, the shed is portable. If you don't like where you've put the shed, simply slide it to another location. If you happen to move from the property, the building can be moved with you; just slide it

PORTABLE GARDEN SHED
MATERIALS LIST

BASE
2   Skids: 4 × 6" × 13'
2   Floor joists (front and rear):
    2 × 6" × 8'
2   Side headers: 2 × 6" × 11'9"
5   Inside floor joists: 2 × 6" × 7'9"
3   Sheets ¾ plywood 4 × 8'

BACK
4   Short studs: 2 × 4 × 45"
3   Long studs: 2 × 4 × 79¾"
1   Bottom plate: 2 × 4" × 8'
2   Center plates: 2 × 4 × 23¼"
2   Upper plates: 2 × 4 × 51"

SIDES
14 Studs: 2 × 4" × 3'9"
2   Bottom plates: 2 × 4" × 11'5"
2   Upper side plates: 2 × 4" × 11'5"

FRONT
6   Short studs: 2 × 4" × 45"
2   Long studs: 2 × 4 × 79¼"
2   Bottom plates: 2 × 4 × 24"
2   Center plates: 2 × 4 × 22¼"
2   Door headers: 2 × 4 × 51"
1   Upper girder: 2 × 6" × 12'
14 Rafters (A): 2 × 4 × 42", cut to fit
14 Rafters (B): 2 × 4 × 29", cut to fit
12 Top braces: 2 × 4 × 24", cut to fit
24 ⅜ plywood truss plates: 6 × 12"
12 ⅜ plywood truss plates: 7¼ × 30"
12 sheets siding
94 linear feet trim: 1 × 4"

DOOR
4   Uprights: 2 × 2 × 80½"
6   Crosspieces: 2 × 2 × 20½"
12 Lag screws: ⅜ × 8"
    Door hardware and hinges

SHINGLES: ⅔ of a square (200 square
    feet of roof area)

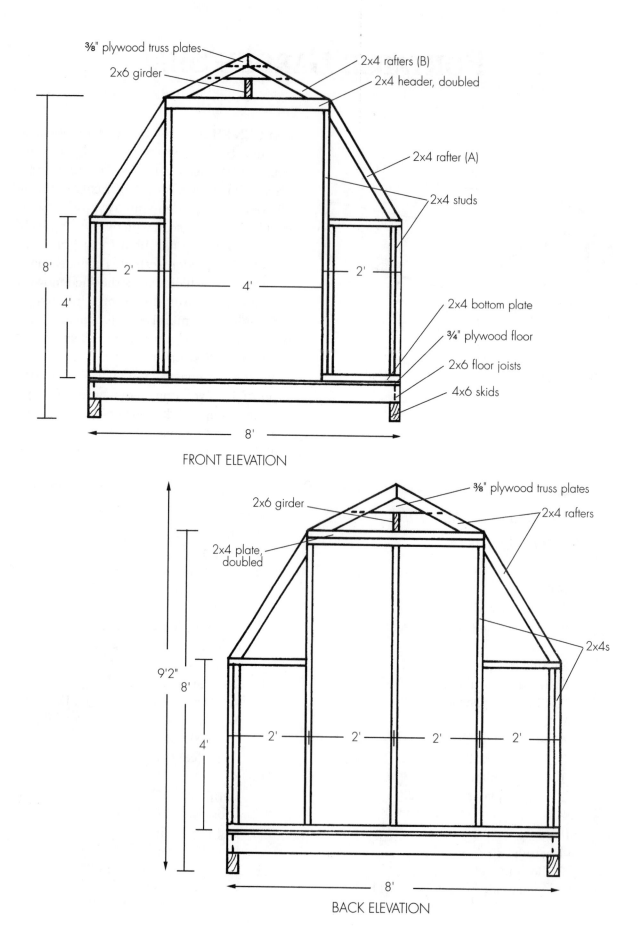

⅜" plywood truss plates

2x6 girder

2x4 rafters (B)

2x4 header, doubled

2x4 rafter (A)

2x4 studs

8'

4'

2'

4'

2'

2x4 bottom plate

¾" plywood floor

2x6 floor joists

4x6 skids

8'

FRONT ELEVATION

⅜" plywood truss plates

2x6 girder

2x4 rafters

2x4 plate, doubled

2x4s

9'2"

8'

4'

2'

2'

2'

2'

8'

BACK ELEVATION

64 Yard & Garden Projects You Can Build Yourself

up on a trailer. And by building on skids, you eliminate footings, foundations, and other expensive permanent supports. I think you'll find the building is fairly economical to construct.

Construction

1. The shed rests on 4x6 skids, so start by cutting the skids to 13-foot lengths. Cut the fronts and backs on a 45-degree bevel so they don't dig in when the structure is pulled or moved. Bore a ¾-inch hole in each end at the front and back. Loops of #9 wire are fastened in each of these holes for a hook-up to a chain you can use to move the building.

2. Position the skids on a smooth surface, spaced 8 feet apart. Cut the front and rear floor joists and anchor them with 8-inch lag screws in counterbored holes down through the top into the skids. Saw the side headers and anchor them with lag screws down into the skids as well, adding more lag screws through the floor joists into each header. It's extremely important to make sure the structure is square at this point. Use a carpenter's square to achieve squareness initially, then measure diagonally from corner to corner. If the diagonal measurements are the same, the structure is square. If not, shift the corners until the measurements are correct.

3. Once the unit is square, position the inside floor joists between the side headers, spaced every two feet on center, and nail solidly with 16d galvanized nails.

4. Position the ¾-inch plywood floor sheets in place and fasten to the headers and floor joists with 8d ring-shank nails.

5. Construct the front end by cutting the pieces to size and then shaping and fastening them together on the plywood platform. Start by cutting the bottom plate. Cut the two long studs and the short outside studs, plus the short center plates. Lay all of these on the platform along with the bottom plate. Note that the bottom plate is cut full length; the opening for the door is cut after the frame is erected.

6. Cut the two 2x4s to form the door header that fits over the door uprights. Nail them together to create a doubled header and put in position.

7. With these pieces laid in place, begin nailing them together with 16d nails. Drive nails through the bottom plate into the door uprights and the outer studs. Hammer through the center plates into the upper ends of the outer studs, then fasten the opposite ends in the proper position with nails through the door uprights. Cut the short "cripple" studs on either side of the door uprights and attach.

8. The door header isn't as thick as the width of the 2x4s, so use shims to hold it up flush with the outside edge of the 2x4s and toe-nail the header in position.

9. Cut two of the lower front rafters (A) to shape and fasten them to the center plates and the headers by toenailing.

10. Cut the upper front rafters (B) to size and shape and cut a ⅜-inch plywood gusset as shown. Nail and glue this (with resorcinol glue) to the backside of the rafter pairs at the top, then toenail the upper rafter assembly to the top of the door headers.

11. Stand the assembled front up on the floor platform and plumb it using a level (check for square with a carpenter's square as well unless you're sure the floor platform is absolutely level). Next, brace the assembly in place with 2x4s nailed to the side studs and back to the side headers.

12. Assemble the rear frame in the same manner, except for the upper section on top of the studs, which utilizes two plates or 2x4s laid flat. Nail the lower in place first and then the upper plate on top of it.

13. The side frames are assembled by cutting a bottom and top plate and the studs to size and shape, and then nailing all of them together on the floor platform. Stand the assembly up and nail the outer end studs on front and back into the studs of the side frames and the bottom plate through the flooring and into the side headers.

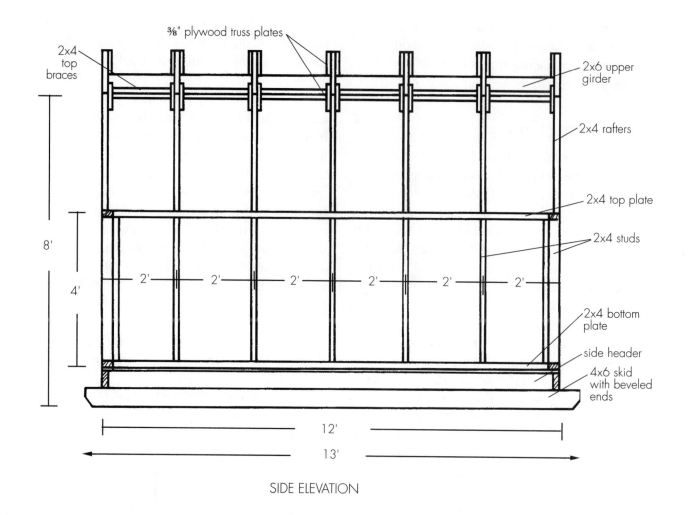

⅜" plywood truss plates

2x4 top braces

2x6 upper girder

2x4 rafters

2x4 top plate

2x4 studs

2x4 bottom plate

side header

4x6 skid with beveled ends

8'

4'

2' 2' 2' 2' 2' 2'

12'

13'

SIDE ELEVATION

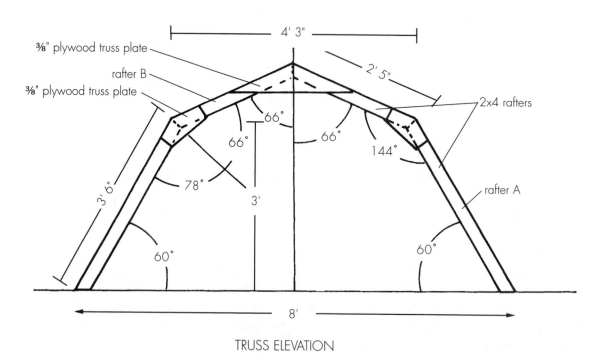

4' 3"

⅜" plywood truss plate

rafter B

⅜" plywood truss plate

2' 5"

66°

66°

66°

66°

144°

2x4 rafters

3' 6"

78°

3'

rafter A

60°

60°

8'

TRUSS ELEVATION

14. Cut the 2×6 upper "girder" and fasten it on top of the front header and rear upper plate by toenailing. Short blocks of wood can also be nailed on either side of it to help provide more strength.

15. The inside rafters are actually trusses that are created by cutting the rafters to the proper shapes and angles as shown in the drawing and fastening them together with ⅜-inch plywood gussets on both sides of each joint. Assemble one truss and then use it as a pattern to assemble the others. You can even stack the pieces on it and fasten them together to ensure all trusses are assembled in the same manner.

16. With a helper, lift the first interior truss and put it down on the girder. Toenail the ends of the truss to the upper top plates and the plywood gussets to the top girder. Install the remaining trusses in the same manner.

17. With all trusses assembled, cut the brace pieces that run between the trusses and attach them.

18. The shed walls can be covered with metal, solid siding, hardboard siding, or plywood. Prefinished hardboard siding or prefinished plywood — such as Georgia Pacific Ply-Bead — are both excellent choices for a quickly covered building. Cut the siding pieces and fasten with 4d galvanized nails into the studs and upper and lower plates. The siding should drop down below the flooring to the bottom edge of the side headers and come up flush with the top edge of the upper plate on the sides.

19. Once the siding has been installed you can add the decorative trim. It's a good idea to paint these in a contrasting color from the siding. Cut the trim to fit first, paint it, and then fasten with galvanized 4d nails.

20. The roof can be metal if you prefer, in which case horizontal purlins are nailed over the rafters. The metal roofing is nailed to the purlins with roofing nails with neoprene washers.

21. In most instances, however, the roof will have a wood decking with shingles. Create the deck with ¼-inch plywood sheathing. Cut the pieces to the correct size and nail them to the rafters, starting at the bottom rafters and using 6d ring-shank nails. Note that the bottom ends should protrude past the wood siding on the walls about 1 inch. Then cut the upper sheathing pieces and nail them in place in the same manner, but remember the sheathing protrudes out flush with the upper trim boards on each end.

22. The next step is to apply asphalt or fiberglass shingles to the roof.

23. Create the double door by nailing plywood siding cut from the door opening to a 2×2 frame as shown. You can nail the (prepainted) decorative trim boards over the door facing.

24. Hang the doors with decorative strap hinges and then install a latch that can be locked from the outside with a padlock.

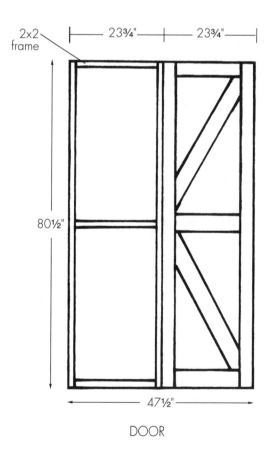

DOOR

OUTDOOR SCREEN

OUTDOOR SCREEN
MATERIALS LIST

- 4   Posts: 4 × 4" × 6'
- 4   Side horizontal supports: 2 × 4 × 48"
- 2   Front horizontal supports: 2 × 4" × 12'
- 1   Center vertical support: 2 × 4 × 33"
- 2   Side lattice panels: 36 × 48"
- 2   Front lattice panels: 36 × 71"
- 1   Center front lower support: 4 × 4", cut to fit

THIS SCREEN is a U-shaped trellis for climbing roses; together they conceal our propane tank. The screen would work equally well to hide garbage cans or heating and air conditioning equipment. Note that the decorative posts used match the surrounding fence posts, and the latticework matches the rose arbor and gate projects also located nearby.

If you prefer to completely conceal an area, solid wood fencing can be used instead of the latticework on this project. The basic construction techniques are the same in both cases. Remember that if you use the screen to hide an air conditioner, the fence must let air circulate easily.

The dimensions of this project are designed to fit my propane tank; you will probably want to customize it to fit what you're screening. Lattice panels come in 4×8 sheets and most lumber is purchased in even increments, so you will make your design easier if you increase your screen's proportions in 2- or 4-foot sections. Remember as well that increased dimensions will also increase your costs.

Construction

Start by laying out the area for the screen and driving stakes in the ground at all four corners. Make absolutely sure you know the exact location of the underground pipe from your propane tank —or even the underground wiring for other equipment — before disturbing the ground by driving stakes or digging post holes.

Of course, it's also important to ensure that the construction is square from the beginning.

Drive two stakes out past the desired corner locations but in line with the sides to create the front. Tie a string between the stakes; they are mini-batter boards. Then drive a stake a couple of inches in front of the string line at the locations for the front posts. Tie string to these and then drive the back stakes in to mark the location of the sidewalls, moving the stakes in and out while using a carpenter's square to ensure the assembly is square and that the post holes are located properly.

The posts are notched to hold the front and

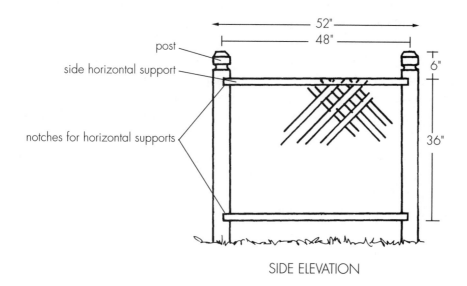

SIDE ELEVATION

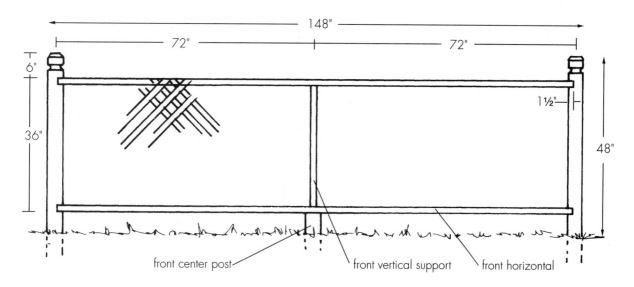

FRONT ELEVATION

side horizontal supports. Rough out these notches to the desired depth (1½ inches) with a portable circular saw. Then use a chisel to chip out the strips and clean up the notches. Shape the post tops if desired.

Dig the post holes and set the front posts, checking carefully that they are correctly spaced and plumb. If you choose to make decorative post tops, make sure they are the correct distance from the ground. Cut the two front horizontal supports and place them in position as you set the posts to assure proper alignment. Toenail in from the sides or top and bottom to anchor them solidly. Set the posts either in concrete or use tamped earth and gravel (see page 2).

Cut the side horizontal supports. Make a 1-inch by 1½-inch notch at the inner edge of the boards to fit into the notches in the front posts and over the front horizontal pieces (see drawing).

Set the rear posts together, slipping the upper and lower side horizontal supports in place at the same time. The posts need to be plumb and the side and front sections must be square with each other. Check for squareness with a carpenter's square before setting the rear posts solidly.

You'll also need a center vertical support, which can be a small center post set in concrete in the ground after the basic framework is completed, but you will have to dig the hole before the front horizontal supports are installed. Or the center support can sit on a 2x6 treated block of wood or a flat concrete block at ground level. Measure, cut, and attach the front vertical support piece.

Next, measure and cut the lattice panels. They protrude 1 inch past the inside edges of the horizontal support pieces at the top and bottom and past the back posts, but are cut flush with the inside edges of the front posts. Cut the front panels first, nail them in place with 4d galvanized nails at the top and bottom, and then cut the two side sections and fasten them in the same manner. An inner support cleat can be ripped from a piece of ¾-inch stock and nailed to the horizontals to provide end support for the inside corners of the latticework at the front posts.

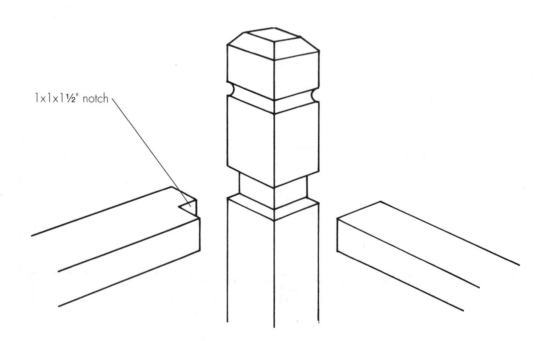

1x1x1½" notch

DETAIL OF NOTCHES IN POST AND BOARD

64 Yard & Garden Projects You Can Build Yourself

Woodshed and Tool Storage Center

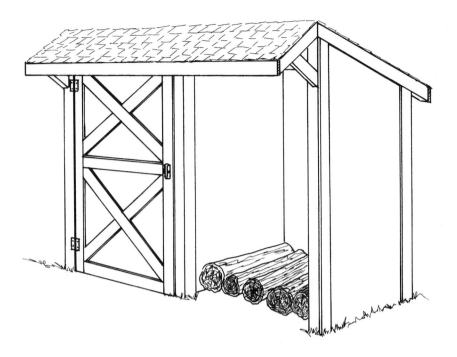

THIS STORAGE CENTER holds firewood as well as rakes, hoes, a push mower, fertilizer, seeds, and all the other assorted gear needed for caring for your lawn and garden. It has two parts: an enclosed and lockable side for tools and an open area for wood storage. It is a

---

Woodshed and Tool Storage Center Materials List

3   Posts: 4 x 4" x 10'
3   Posts: 4 x 4" x 8'
1   Front upper girt: 2 x 4" x 8'
1   Front lower girt: 2 x 4" x 7'9"
3   Rear girts: 2 x 4" x 8'
6   Side girts: 2 x 4" x 34½"
6   Inside side girts: 2 x 4 x 34½"
3   Inside back girts: 2 x 4" x 3'9"
3   Floor supporting girts: 2 x 4 x 41½"
Floor: ¾ plywood x 41½" x 4'
2   Center and left front trim strips:
      1 x 5 x 6'8"
1   Left upper front trim strip: 1 x 5 x 16"
1   Right lower front trim strip:
      1 x 7¼" x 6'8"

1   Right upper front trim strip:
      1 x 7¼ x 16"
2   Top plates: 2 x 4" x 8'
5   Rear rafters: 2 x 4" x 5'3"
5   Front rafters: 2 x 4" x 2'3"
5   Gussets: ½ plywood x 6 x 12"
2   Side front braces: 2 x 4" x 25",
      cut to fit
2   Fascia boards: 1 x 4" x 8'
8   Siding sheets: 4 x 8' sheets, plywood
      or prefinished hardboard
Door framing: 22 linear feet of 2x2s
Door trim: 40 linear feet of 1x4s
3   Roof decking: ⅜" x 4 x 8' sheets
Shingles: 64 square feet
Hardware, door hinges, and latch

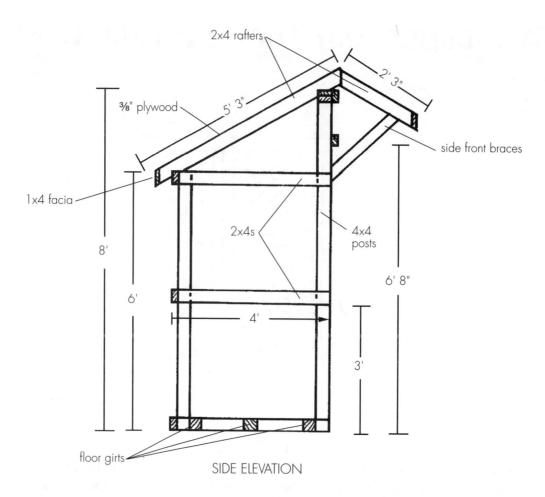

2x4 rafters

3⁄8" plywood

2' 3"

5' 3"

side front braces

1x4 facia

2x4s

4x4 posts

8'

6' 8"

6'

4'

3'

floor girts

SIDE ELEVATION

permanent structure utilizing pole building techniques that are easy even for a beginning carpenter. A wooden floor in the storage area provides pest-free storage, while the woodshed end is open to the ground.

Construction

Start by determining the exact site for the building and marking the post locations. Make sure the posts will not interfere with any utility lines or underground cables. To lay out the building, measure the approximate distance for each of the four corners according to the plans and drive stakes for the rough location of each post center. Remember, the post centers will be approximately 3 inches inside the perimeter of the building. To ensure the building is square, measure diagonally from stake to stake. The diagonal measurements should be the same. If they are not, move the stakes un-

til they are equal and still maintain the proper measurements for the sides, front, and back.

Dig the holes for the posts (a local building supply center or an Extension agent can tell you how deep), allowing for the depth of the post embedment plus 4 inches for a layer of gravel or concrete. The holes should be twice the width of the posts. The posts can be set in concrete or (in most parts of the country) tamped earth and gravel, depending on your local soil conditions. Concrete is the most expensive embedment method but lasts the longest. On the other hand, gravel and tamped earth will usually suffice for a building of this size (see page 2 for more on setting posts).

To set the posts in concrete pour a 4-inch punch pad in the bottom of each hole and let them cure for twenty-four hours before setting the posts.

Position the posts using 2x4 braces to hold them in the proper location and keep them

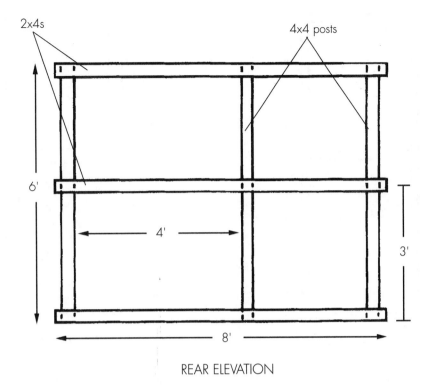

2x4s

4x4 posts

6'

4'

3'

8'

REAR ELEVATION

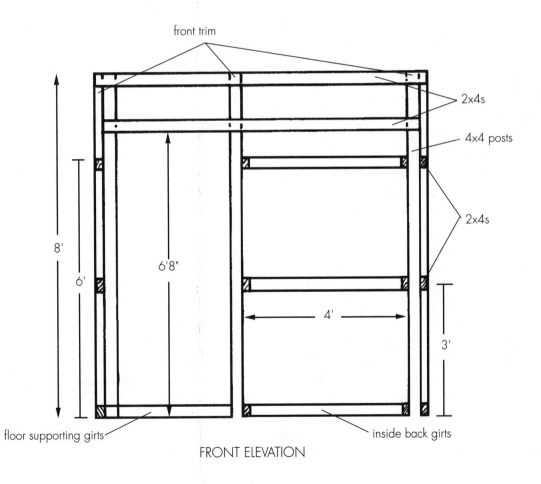

front trim

2x4s

4x4 posts

2x4s

8'

6'

6'8"

4'

3'

floor supporting girts

inside back girts

FRONT ELEVATION

151

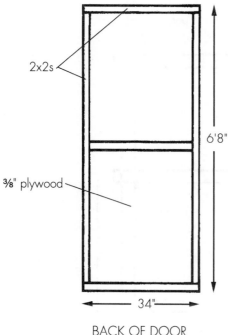

2x2s

⅜" plywood

6'8"

34"

BACK OF DOOR

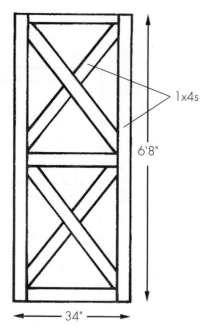

1x4s

6'8"

34"

FRONT OF DOOR

plumb. A long carpenter's level can plumb them in both directions (their two outer sides). Again, measure the diagonals to check for squareness. You can also run a string line around the perimeter, level it with a long level, and compare the dimensions of opposite sides.

For the small amount of concrete used for this project you can probably use premixed concrete that comes in a bag with sand and gravel. Simply add water and pour the mixture in the hole around the braced and supported posts. Round the concrete up around the posts and smooth it down so water will run away from the posts rather then settle in against them.

Tamped-earth posts are erected in much the same manner, except that a layer of gravel is placed in the hole before the posts are positioned in place and plumbed. Next, a layer of earth and then a layer of gravel are shoveled in the hole around the posts and tamped solidly. Then another layer of soil and another of gravel are added and tamped. This process is repeated until the hole is filled and the post anchored solidly in place.

Use a straightedge such as a long 2x4 and a level to mark across from the shortest rear post and cut the other rear posts to the correct

height using a handsaw or chain saw. Do the same for the front posts.

Cut the short side horizontal girts and nail them to the posts enclosing the tool storage area on both the outside and inside walls. Then cut and nail the long rear horizontal girts across the rear posts with 16d nails. Saw and fasten the top plate for the front wall, nailing the front top girt and the post fronts to it. Cut the bottom floor supporting girts and attach one in front, one in back, and one in the center.

The rafters supporting the cantilevered roof are actually trusses formed by gluing and nailing plywood gussets to the eave joints of the two rafters. Cut the rafters to the proper length, cut a notch in both the lower and upper ends of the long rafters, and join the rafters together to create the trusses. Position a rafter truss on one end of the building and nail it securely through the notch and into the back top girt and the top plate with 16d nails. Fasten the remaining rafters in the same manner. Nail the fascia boards on the front edges of the rear and front rafters. Finally, nail the side front roof braces in position.

The building can be covered with any number of siding types. The simplest and fastest siding is probably either prefinished hardboard siding such as Masonite or plywood siding such as Georgia Pacific Ply-Bead, which gives the appearance of tongue-and-groove planking.

Start covering the building by fastening back pieces in place first, then the ends. Make sure you get the first sheet plumb so the second sheet will fit properly. Nail the inside sheets in the same manner. Cut outside trim pieces to cover the rough edges of the siding and to fill the open area at the front post. Use the narrower trim stock for the other areas or make all the trim wider if you desire.

Cover the rafters with ⅜-inch plywood sheathing nailed with 3d or 4d ring-shank nails. Shingle the roof to match existing architecture.

The door is a 2×2 frame made by ripping the 2×2s from 2×4 stock with a portable circular saw with a ripping guide or a table or radial arm saw. Nail plywood siding to the frame before ripping trim strips for the outside edges of the front of the door.

You can hang the door with butt hinges, but strap hinges are more decorative. Then add a hasp and padlock as well as a door handle and you're in business.

If you are not using prefinished siding, paint the shed to suit. You may prefer to paint the trim and upper "fake" rafter boards a contrasting color. In this case, it's easier to paint them before fastening and after painting the entire building the proper base color.

STEPPING-OFF RAFTERS

The most accurate way to mark rafters for cutting is to use a rafter square and "step-off" the rafter, using the square to represent the rise and run of the roof pitch. Since the square forms a right triangle, like the imaginary rise and run of the roof, use the scale on the small blade (the *tongue*), to represent the roof's rise and the scale on the large blade (the *body*), to represent the run.

As an example, we'll mark off a rafter with a total run of 12 feet 3 inches, a rise of 6 feet 1½ inches, and an overhang of 1 foot 8 inches. Dividing the rise by the run, we see that this is a perfect 6 in 12 roof. First, select the straightest piece of rafter stock you have to use for the pattern. With the rafter up on sawhorses, locate the 12-inch mark on the body of the square and position it against the edge of the rafter at one end. Locate the number for the unit of rise, in this case 6, on the tongue of the square and position it against the edge. Draw a line along the back of the tongue to mark the top plumb cut at the centerline of the ridge. When this is cut you will have to subtract half the thickness of the ridge plate from this line to compensate for the thickness of the plate.

To begin stepping-off the rafter, first measure off the odd unit of run, in this case 3 inches. With the square in the original position, measure off 3 inches on the body and make a mark on the rafter. Slide the square down the rafter, holding the 6 in 12 position, until the back of the tongue is on the 3-inch mark you made. Now mark a line along the back of the tongue and body. Once you have marked off the odd unit of run, you are ready to move the square down the rafter in the 6 in 12 position until the 6-inch mark on the tongue lines up with the previous 12-inch mark on the body. Step the rafter off 12 times in this manner to measure the 12 feet of run. Your last mark will indicate the entire length of the rafter from the centerline of the ridge to the outside of the wall plate.

To mark the bird's mouth cut that will sit on the wall plate, turn the square upside down and position the 12-inch mark on the body at the top of the last plumb line and the 6-inch mark on the tongue on the rafter's upper edge. The horizontal line along the bottom of the body marks the bird's-mouth cut. Finally, two more steps can be made with the square in its upside-down position, one full 12-inch step and another 8-inch step. This will give you the 1-foot, 8-inch overhang for the eaves. Make the tail cut, then return to the ridge and make the top plumb cut. Remember to shorten the rafter by one-half the thickness of the ridge plate.

A Guide to Garden & Backyard Fencing

Decorative fencing can combine many elements to provide an attractive and practical fence.

ONE OF THE MOST COMMON and varied garden and backyard projects is fencing. Fencing designs can be plain and simple or fancy depending on what the fencing is needed for, the surrounding landscaping or architectural style, your cost requirements, and the amount of time and labor you wish to invest.

To choose your fencing you must first determine your needs. Do you want a fence to keep pets and small children in your yard? Do you need to be able to see through the fence? Or do you want a fence to contain some kind

of livestock? In this section, I've described some basic types of fencing that will give you an idea of the options. You may want to use one as shown, or modify a design. At the very least, you can use some of the general fencing techniques described to construct whatever type you choose.

Once you determine the type of fence you need, measure along the lines you want your fencing to run (a good 100-foot steel tape is invaluable for longer spans) before making up a plan illustrating the layout. This should include measurements for post spacing, places for gates, and problem areas such as sloping ground. A plan will also help you make up a materials list. Before you get started, make sure to check local building codes as well. When building along a property line, be certain your fence is actually on your property; more than one landowner has had to tear down and rebuild a fence because it was constructed on their neighbor's property. Try to determine the location of all underground phone, power, water, and gas lines in the area you will be fencing to avoid disrupting your utilities, endangering yourself, or having to re-plan your fencing because of a badly placed post hole.

My grandfather had just one thing to say about fences: "Build them good, or you'll build them again." That pretty much sums up my attitude, too. Don't scrimp on materials or labor or you'll pay later.

Enclosures for Small Children and Pets

Commercial chain-link fencing with all its components can be purchased at most major building supply dealers and is good for containing small children and most dogs. Children can't climb it easily, and dogs can't wiggle through or force openings as they can with other types of mesh fencing. The components consist of metal posts, metal top and bottom fence supports, various connectors, and the actual chain link fencing, which is applied to the completed framework. Matching manufactured gates are also available.

The construction process is fairly simple and straightforward, with full instructions usually included with the components. The key is to have properly spaced posts that are plumb and anchored in concrete.

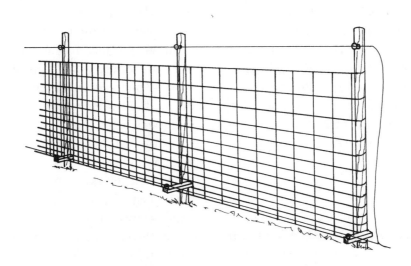

GARDEN FENCING

FENCING TO PROTECT a garden from wandering pets, scratching chickens, livestock, and other nuisances requires less strength than height. For instance, 4-inch round poles, 4×4 posts, or even steel posts with wooden corner posts are often used with 4- or 6-foot-wide hog wire or wire mesh to enclose gardens. Such fences also make great trellises for plants such as cucumbers and climbing beans.

But, there are two critters that require a great deal more thought and effort to keep out of the garden than pets and chickens: deer and raccoons. I've been battling them — like many other rural landowners have — for years. Deer can jump incredible heights, so a deer-proof fence requires a 12-foot-high wall. And deer aren't just a problem in the country anymore; many towns, cities, and suburbs face growing deer problems as well. Raccoons, on the other hand, can climb anything that doesn't move — and some things that do, as more than one old-time coon hunter can attest. Folks have tried almost anything you can come up with in their battle with these critters. We always put out about a half-acre of sweet corn, and for many years I have tried different tactics to keep the raccoons from enjoying most of the sweet corn before we get our chance to.

We finally settled on a double strand of electric wire, and for the past few years we've had a lot fewer problems with raccoons and deer, even though we've been seeing more and more deer in the orchard next to the garden. The wires are positioned so that the lower one is approximately 6 inches off the ground and the higher one 4 feet. I use uninsulated plastic posts and wooden posts with electric wire supports. Even though deer could easily jump the fence they seem to sense the danger and stay away from it. Once or twice I've had a deer bust the fence during the night, but other than that it was left alone entirely.

Materials

Your garden fence can be constructed with wood posts or, as is more common, round poles. You can also use wood posts for the corners and steel posts between, or even just steel posts. The posts can be placed in holes bored or dug in the ground and anchored with tamped earth, a combination of earth and gravel, a combination of concrete and earth, or with a full concrete embedment (see page 2 for more on pole embedment). Fence posts up to 6 inches in diameter can be driven in place with tractor-powered post drivers. What-

ever you use to drive the posts, those with diameters larger than 4 inches should be pointed for best results.

Fence posts can and often are made of native materials. Thousands of miles of fencing here in the Ozarks have fence posts of Osage orange or cedar, and many of the old Osage orange posts are still standing after half a century. Today, most wooden fence posts are manufactured. If you choose manufactured wooden posts, they must be pressure-treated wood and labeled as acceptable for in-ground contact.

Construction

A good fence is only as good as the corner posts that anchor it in place. An anecdote from my youth sums up the importance of strong corner posts. My parents' home sat directly at an intersection. The neighbor across the road decided to put in a new fence. As my brother and I played in the front yard, we watched a farm worker just across the road dig a hole over 6 feet deep and almost 4 feet across. He worked on the hole for almost three days and during the last day all we could see was dirt and rocks being flung out of the hole. That afternoon the landowner grunted with satisfaction as he looked over the hole. The next day, a half-dozen workers hauled over the giant post — a 12-foot-long and 3-foot-wide trunk section from a giant Osage orange tree — and began constructing a tripod to hang a rope-and-pulley lift, which required almost another full day's work. The following day, after much discussion and more planning, the giant post was finally hoisted high in the air and lowered carefully into the hole. Then began the concrete work. The remainder of that day was taken up with mixing and pouring concrete in and around the post. By the following day the concrete had set and the remainder of the fence was started.

Fifteen years later while my family was

eating dinner, we heard the sounds of sliding tires, crunching metal, and breaking glass. We ran outside and found a driver had missed the turn and hit the post at about 50 miles per hour. Despite a totaled car (and a seriously injured person), the post hadn't shifted 1 inch and the few wires that were yet attached were still taunt. That post remains standing forty years later.

Several methods are used to create corner posts, but the most common methods use either two or three posts. Two posts work for short runs, but three posts are best for longer runs. Three posts are more costly in both materials and time.

A corner post should be a minimum of 6 inches in diameter and brace posts a minimum of 4 inches. Brace posts are normally 8 feet long with about 42 inches buried, which leaves 54 inches for the post above ground. The brace posts are spaced 8 feet from the corner posts; with the three-post system, the third post is 8 feet from the second. A 4x4 horizontal brace is placed between each set of posts.

One common method of supporting the braces is to cut notches in the posts about 12 inches down from the top of each post to receive the horizontal braces. A better method is to bore holes in the posts and the ends of the horizontal braces and insert steel rods cut from reinforcing rod. The ends of the horizontal pieces can be toenailed into the posts for added support.

Four strands of #9 galvanized wire are wrapped into a loop from the top of one post diagonally to the bottom of the next and then twisted taut using a stick or short section of pipe. With 1-inch pipe you can twist the wire and then pull the pipe out (you'll have to leave the stick). Next, a second diagonal wire is positioned to cross the first, creating a solid support that will resist tension from the fence. You may wish to provide added support with a ground anchor that runs off the corner support posts in line with the fencing. A corner post needs two ground anchors.

Begin laying out the fence by placing stakes at each end with a string line between them.

Setting the Posts

It's a good idea to completely clean all brush and debris from the site of your planned fence and to level the ground as much as possible before beginning construction. After you've set the corner and end posts, lay out the rest of the fence before you get busy setting all the fence posts. You can do this by stetching a string line or single strand of wire stretched fairly taut at the bottom of the posts to indicate the fence line. If you don't do this on straight runs first, you may place the second and third brace posts out of line. If you're installing a contour fence that has curves in it, lay out a smooth curve with stakes and a string line from each corner or end post.

Dig the post holes at their proper spacing before positioning the posts in place against the string line and plumbing them in all directions.

Secure the posts by embedding them in concrete, tamped earth, and/or gravel around their bases.

As my childhood story indicates, properly setting the posts — particularly the corner, end, and brace posts — is the key to a long-lasting and useful fence. You can dig your post holes with either a hand-operated post digger or with a power digger. Hand diggers come in either auger and clam-shell types, and power diggers can be either a small-engine-driven style or tractor-powered models. Tractor-powered diggers are best for large fencing jobs. In most areas you should be able to rent or hire a power digger.

Your post holes should be at least twice the diameter of your posts. When you need additional strength, such as when a post must support a gate, pouring concrete around the post is a good reinforcement tactic. There are two ways to add the concrete. The simplest is

excellent for out-of-the-way places where it might be difficult to mix concrete. Tamp earth around the bottom of the post to hold it in position or brace it in place with 2×4s. Then pour a dry sack of Sakrete (which contains sand and gravel as well as Portland cement) around the post. Fill the remaining hole with soil. In a day or two the moisture from the soil will set the post solidly in place.

The single best method to get a rock-solid corner post, however, is to set it in concrete you've mixed up on-site. Allow the concrete to set up overnight or twenty-four hours before stretching fence from it.

On brace posts as well as other wooden posts, I've found base rock to be an ideal substitute for concrete. Since it is made to be a base for a roadbed, it consists of both small and large substrate. Once wet, base rock packs almost as hard as concrete.

My farm is located on an Ozark hilltop and what topsoil is left is mostly red clay. I've found that an excellent mixture for most posts is created by placing a layer of clay in the bottom around the post, adding a layer of base rock, and then tamping these down solid. You next add another layer of clay, another layer of base rock, and again tamp until solid. Continue this process until the hole around the post is filled and you have a solid, secure post.

Regardless of the embedment method used, make sure all posts are plumb before setting them solidly. Contour posts are an exception here, but they will be discussed later.

Stretcher posts should be set at any abrupt change in fence direction, at the edges of ditches or gullies, and at various distances along a long fence run as well as corner and end posts. For flat, even ground the spacing is usually 40 rods (1 rod is equal to 5½ yards or 16½ feet), but for uneven terrain spacing them every 20 rods is a better choice. My corner and end posts are usually 8 feet long and at least 4 inches in diameter. My braces are usually a square 4 inches wide on each side and 8 feet long. The braces are placed between the posts — again, using notches or steel rods — and then I run the diagonal wires and twist them taut.

Once all end, corner, and stretcher posts are set, a string line or a temporary section of wire is established from end to end (or corner to corner) and the line posts put in place. Whether you drive or dig holes for your line posts, their usual spacing is 1 rod, but they can be set more closely if an especially strong fence is desired.

These days steel posts are often used for the line posts. Steel posts are long lasting, easily driven, and special wire clips make fastening wire to them fairly easy.

Steel posts can be driven in the ground using a power driver on a tractor, but they are usually fairly easy to drive using a special post driver. You can purchase one or, if

PROBLEM POSTS

Sometimes, as with ledge rock, it just isn't possible to get a post deep enough in the ground. In such cases, earth anchors are used, which are metal rods with a large screw on one end and a screw eye on the opposite end. They are screwed in as close to the post as possible and the post is wired down to them, using a lever.

you're handy with a welder, you can make your own easily.

When using steel posts, remember to get them plumb and, more importantly, lined up properly with their attaching side (the one with the bumps) facing the fence wires. If the side is not lined up correctly, the connecting wires won't fit easily and you'll probably end up saying a few blue words or so before you get the wires attached.

Once the line posts are set, it's time to stretch the fence wire. To stretch hog wire you'll need a fence clamp, which can easily be made as shown on page 21.

Stretching Hog or Woven Wire

With one end of the wire anchored firmly to one end post, attach the fence clamp to the area you will stretch to, such as the first stretcher post. Attach a fence stretcher or come-along to the second stretcher or corner post, or set up a temporary stretcher post with a diagonal wooden brace. I've also used my tractor bucket several times as an "anchor" for fence stretching. The fence stretcher must be anchored at the same height as the clamp. It's a dangerous mistake to use an automobile or tractor to pull the fence, as the wire can break and curl back with a fast snap, possibly causing injury or damage.

Stretch only a little at a time, then walk the fence line and pick up or rearrange the wire, unhooking it from the posts where it inevitably catches and removing any kinks. Try to keep the hog wire as vertical as possible, with neither the bottom nor top ahead of the other.

In most instances, the wire should be stretched until the "tension curves" built into the horizontal wires are pulled to about one-half their original height.

With the wire stretched and in place, begin stapling at the first brace post. Staple the bottom first to position the fence at ground level and then at the top to ensure it is stretched vertically as much as desired. Finally, fasten the line wires in between.

At the end of the run, staple the wires to the last post and then cut the wire using fencing pliers; leave enough to wrap the wire completely around the post and twist around the stretched line wires. Then wrap the line wires in place and add double staples on both ends. If you're not at the end of the run, merely staple in place, unfasten the fence clamp, and move on to the next run.

Contour Fencing

Not all fence runs are perfectly straight. When fencing must be run on a contour or curve, use stakes to establish a smooth, gentle curve. The stakes are normally placed 1 rod apart. Run a string line around the stakes to ensure the curve is gentle and no individual stake protrudes out further than the line of curvature.

Contour posts should lean at the top about 2 inches away from the direction you will be stretching. When the fence is stretched the posts will tend to lean back into a plumb position due to the tension.

Wire for a contour fence should be stretched only about one-half to two-thirds as tightly as a fence with a straight line. Less tension should be applied to the sharper curves. A common problem on contour fencing is that the wire easily catches on the posts as it is stretched. You'll have to stretch a little, then walk the line and uncatch the wire, before stretching more.

DECORATIVE FARM FENCING

IF YOUR PRIMARY NEED for fencing is decoration, then you have enormous freedom of design. Decorative farm and garden fencing styles range from simple board-on-post fences — commonly seen in the beautiful thoroughbred country around Louisville, Kentucky — to elaborate picket fences, which is an old style returning with vigor in contemporary design schemes.

Even the ordinary board-on-post farm fence used to finish and show off a farm drive or showcase a beautiful farm pasture can be embellished with a bit of the unusual. The fence shown below, which lines our drive and front pasture, is an example of how a little extra work can give you a more interesting and attractive farm fence.

This fence was constructed of 4x4 pressure-treated posts spaced 8 feet apart with 16-foot-long treated 2x6s for the horizontal boards. Several years before I had constructed a similar fence of untreated 1x6s. The boards

DECORATIVE FARM FENCING MATERIALS LIST

Posts: 4 x 4" x 6', spaced 8' on center
4 Boards to a section: 2 x 6" x 16'

eventually bowed in and out; youngsters climbing on them and horses bending over them meant I had a short-lived and expensive fence. So I settled on the thicker materials the next time.

Construction

The shaped post tops look complicated but are actually quite easy to make. Chamfering gives a finished look to the posts and also helps drain rainwater off the posts quicker. To make the chamfers, simply mark 1 inch down from each post top and then use a square to

Fence post tops can easily be made quite decorative.

mark a line all around the post top at that measurement. With a portable circular saw set at 45 degrees, cut the chamfer following your line.

The decorative groove is formed with a ⅝-inch half-round router bit and a heavy-duty router. Pencil in a mark 6½ inches below the post top. Now clamp a straight piece of 1×2 to the post positioned on the mark and push the router across the post guided by the board. Don't force the router too much if it slows. In some instances, it may take several passes to get the cut to the proper depth without burning the wood with the router bit.

Incidentally, I made marks for the chamfer, the groove, and the board spacing from the top down on one side of each post, as well as the approximate depth it would set in the ground (in this case, 2 feet). Doing the complete layout at once helps ensure accuracy.

Setting the Posts

It is especially important to properly set posts for decorative fencing. Five very important factors are involved: the posts must be set absolutely plumb; the posts must all be in a straight line; the flat sides of the posts must align with the fence line; the post tops must all be the same distance from ground level; and,

most important, the posts must all be spaced the correct distance. If the spacing isn't done exactly, the boards won't fit across the posts properly.

The first step is to lay out the fence with stakes and then run a string between the end stakes. Decorative fencing can be constructed in a straight or curved line. You can also follow a contoured slope — if it is fairly gentle. I utilized a 45-degree corner in one section so the fence wouldn't protrude into the driveway with a sharp, square corner. Once the fence outline is determined by the string, use a tape measure and stakes to locate each of the posts. Normally posts for this type of fence are placed in holes, and marking the holes precisely is extremely important. It's quite frustrating to dig a series of holes only to discover you started off incorrectly and need to shift some or even all of the holes to meet the fence line.

The depth of the holes depends on the fence height, as follows:

Fence Height	Hole Depth for Posts
3 to 5 feet	2 feet
6 feet	2½ feet
8 feet	3½ feet

These decorative post tops are cut on a 45-degree angle to form a chamfer. Then use a half-round router bit to cut a groove around the upper portion of the posts.

Fences of this type also require that the posts be set solidly. Again, several methods can be used: solid concrete embedment, tamped soil, or tamped soil and base rock. If using concrete, pour a layer first, allow it to set, and then position the post on the first layer and pour concrete around it. Another good technique is to allow the post to sit on the earth, position steel reinforcing rods through the post, and pour concrete around this assembly. These tactics allow water to drain down and away from posts; if the post is totally enclosed in concrete, water can end up being trapped. If your soil is loose and sandy or if the fence must stand against strong winds, a cross-T of cleats nailed to the post bottom that is surrounded by tamped earth can be used.

Set the end or corner posts first. Make sure they are in the correct position and are perfectly plumb in both directions. After final post placement and before the concrete or tamped earth sets up, recheck for plumb. If the posts tend to shift, brace them in place temporarily.

Since I often have to do a lot of building chores alone, I've worked out several ways to handle most work by myself. For instance, in order to determine the exact spacing for the posts I run a string line at the bottom and top of the end or corner posts. Next, I drive a nail in the first post at each string level line and tie a short piece of string tautly around both top and bottom strings. I then hook the tape measure on a nail on the first post and pull the tape along the string until I reach the proper measurement. The string knots are slid along to these points. I not only get a center measurement for post placement but an estimate of plumb. When starting with the end or corner posts, merely hook the tape measure over the edge of the post first.

Although a string and string line level can be used to create a level line, the fence boards will not look perfectly level on a sloping ground. To correct this, set the posts with the same height protruding from ground level. In the case of the fence shown, the posts tops

If boards are warped or twisted, clamps can be used to pull them tightly into position before nailing.

The horizontal boards are attached to the posts easily with a cordless nailer.

were all placed 48 inches above ground level, which meant either adjusting the depth of each post hole or cutting the bottoms of posts off at the measurement needed.

In any case, the posts are positioned with their front edges just touching the strings at their top and bottom and with the center of the posts on the marking tie strings indicating the proper distance from the previous post. The posts are then set using whatever embedment method you desire. Before their final placement, check with a level to ensure they are plumb and remeasure your spacing to make sure they're in the proper position.

If you use tamped earth or tamped earth and base rock to set the posts, you can start applying horizontal boards or rails immediately. With concrete, the posts must set twenty-four hours before applying the boards.

Boards may be applied in several different patterns. The accompanying drawings show straight horizontal, X, and zigzag patterns. For a combination decorative and livestock fence,

the straight horizontal is the best choice as some animals can get their heads caught in the more open designs.

A trick I've used for years when installing the long boards by myself is to drive 16d nails partially in the post at the correct height to support both ends of a board. I then pick a board up, place it on the nails, fasten the first end in place, and go to the second end and attach it. Finally, I pull out both of the supporting nails. The boards should be fastened

STRAIGHT HORIZONTAL PATTERN

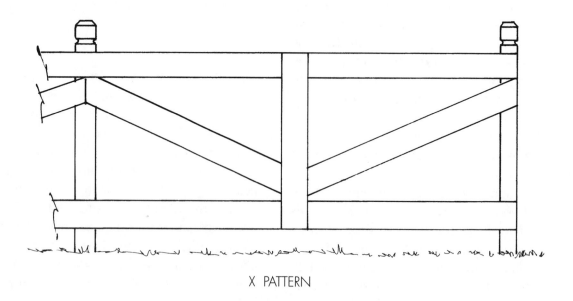

X PATTERN

to the posts with 16d galvanized nails.

What about twisted boards? Twisting often happens if treated lumber is stacked outdoors before it can be installed. To correct this, fasten one end solidly with galvanized 16d ring-shank nails, then use a big bar clamp to pull the opposite end up snugly and anchor it with the ring-shanks.

One of the most useful tools I've discovered for outdoor projects — particularly projects like fences that require driving a lot of big nails — is the ITW Paslode Impulse cordless nailer. You can fasten boards for even a long fence in a matter of minutes. I tack-nail the boards in position with just one nail in each post. Once I get a section or run completed to my satisfaction, I go back and nail solidly with the nailer.

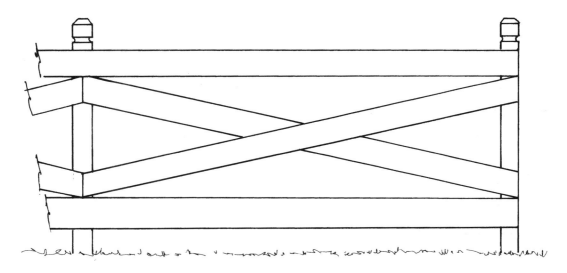

ZIGZAG PATTERN

WOOD-RAIL FENCING

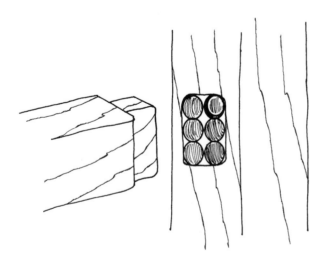

BORING HOLES

WOOD-RAIL FENCES are quite popular in many parts of the country and can occasionally be used as cattle and horse fencing as well as decorative fencing. Rail fences are often purchased in sections as a kit, but you can also make your own.

Begin by making up a "package" of parts just as if you were purchasing a kit fence. Cut all rails to the proper length, shaping the tenons on their ends using a drawknife or hatchet. Cut the posts to the proper length and round their tops so rainwater will drain. Bore holes for the rail tenons using a fitted "expansion" bit in a hand-cranked brace and bit. An expansion bit is simply a bit that is adjustable and can bore holes in any diameter within a given range. You should also bore holes for the gate hangers in the posts and gate uprights.

Assemble each section completely. Start by placing the first post in concrete and allowing it to set up. Then put together a section of rails that includes the first preset post and a second post. Allow that post to set up and proceed to the next section. As you can see, this is an easy step-by-step project that can be done over several weekends. Once all pieces have been assembled, you can strengthen the fence further by adding 3-inch lag screws in the joints.

Make up the gates in the same manner. Remember to bolt the diagonal brace after ensuring the gate is square. Hang the gate by lifting it up and fitting the open hangers down over the upright retainers of the post hangers. Note that the diagonal is notched to fit into the gate uprights and around the gate horizontal as well.

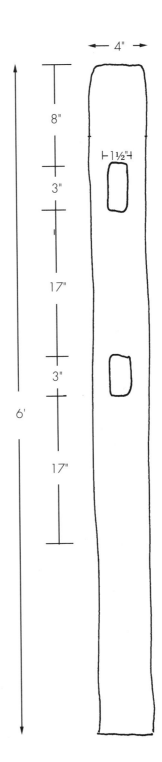

WOOD-RAIL FENCE POST, ROUNDED TOP AND HOLES FOR RAIL TENONS

SPLIT-RAIL FENCING

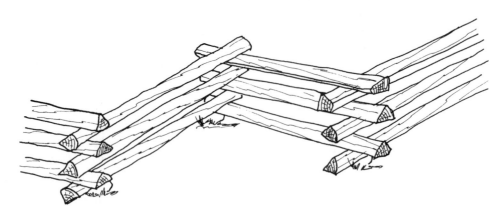

You can easily build your own split-rail fence to beautify your home — it's a great way of utilizing small trees that need to be thinned from a woodlot. After the logs have been split, it's merely a matter of stacking overlapping logs in a zigzag fashion until you reach the height and fence length you desire.

SPLIT-RAIL FENCES are a part of an old tradition in America. A split-rail fence can also act as a background for a flower bed with the area between the zigzags creating planting pockets. The rustic look will blend with almost any type of informal setting.

Building the fence is very simple once you have the rails on hand. Sometimes you can purchase the rails from building or garden supply outlets in larger cities. An alternative, however, is to utilize young trees that must be thinned from a woodlot, whether your own or someone else's. These days most private woodlot owners are conscious of proper woodland management and spend some time each year thinning out unwanted trees to give the better-quality trees more space to grow properly. Since thinning is also a necessity in most national and state forests across the country, you may be able to obtain a permit to cut cull timber on government land. Check with the local forestry department to see what is available in your area. In most instances, you will be restricted to trees that are marked for removal. You must also follow rules for proper cutting procedures and for removing or stacking limbs for brush piles.

Materials

The best logs will be between 8 and 12 inches in diameter at their small end. Logs should be 8 to 10 feet in length, with 8 feet being the most popular size.

Oak, walnut, Osage orange, and cedar split easily. Some woods that are tough to split are hickory and elm. Green and freshly cut logs will split much more easily than seasoned logs, and logs cut in the cold of winter will split easier than those cut in the spring of the year when the sap is rising. Your logs should be free of knots or branches or they will not split cleanly and may twist and turn around each knot.

The only tools needed are a couple of metal splitting wedges, a heavy-duty splitting maul, and a pair of safety goggles or glasses. You may also wish to wear a pair of leather gloves to protect your hands, sturdy boots to protect your feet, and long pants and a long-sleeved shirt.

Good splitting mauls are heavy, with an angled wedge on one side and a face side to drive steel wedges into the wood on the other. The angled side is itself used for splitting. I would suggest getting a maul with a fiberglass handle since wooden handles break more often.

Splitting Rails

Splitting rails can be easy or hard, depending on how you approach it. My Uncle Mike, an old-timer who used to split rails for a living, knew that wood could be very tenacious but —with patience—could be worked quite simply.

The first step is to start one of the wedges directly in the center of the small end of the log using the maul or a short-handled sledge. Once the wedge will stay in place, use the maul to drive it as far into the end of the log as possible, creating a wide split.

Take the second wedge and drive it down in the split started in the side of the log. It should be positioned no further than 12 to 18 inches from the end of the first wedge. Drive it until the first wedge becomes loosened. Remove the first wedge and continue driving the second wedge in place until it is buried in the log. Then simply leapfrog the first wedge into the split created by the second wedge (position 3 in drawing) and drive it in; repeat this process until the log splits out. With a bit of experience you can drive the first and second wedges in place and then use a splitting maul to finish out the split. It usually takes less than five minutes to split a normal log, either

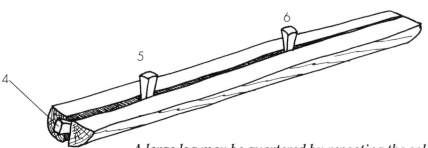

The first step in making rails is to saw logs to the correct length. Start a steel or wooden wedge in one end of the log. (Wear safety glasses during this process.) Use a heavy maul or sledge to drive the wedge as far as possible into the log. Drive a second wedge into the crack you created until the crack widens enough to loosen the first wedge. You then merely leapfrog the wedges up the crack, moving wedge 1 into the wedge 3 position, until the entire log splits.

A large log may be quartered by repeating the splitting process on half a log.

way. You can also use this process to split the halves into quarters which will split much easier.

If the wood starts to split off to one side rather than going straight down the center to the other end of the log, remove the wedges and start from the opposite end to bring the split ends back together.

Another problem that may occur is that the halves of a particularly tough piece of wood may spring back together, making the wedge jump back out of the split when it is hit with the maul. In this case, turn the log over and drive the wedge in from the opposite side of the split. This will almost always alleviate the problem.

Once your logs are split, position a flat rock on the ground for each junction and start stacking up logs to finish the fence. With a little practice you'll find that making split-rail fencing is fun and easy and a great way of utilizing what would otherwise be burned as firewood. But then, if you get tired of your fence you can always burn your now dried and cured logs.

PICKET FENCING

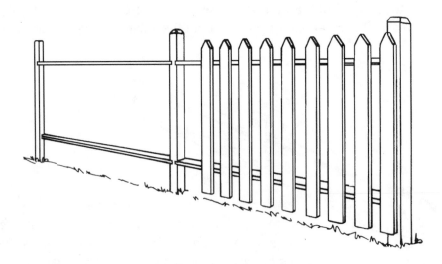

SYNONYMOUS with beautiful yards and gardens, picket fencing is a very personal and decorative way to create a focus for landscaping. With a little time and the proper tools, it's also fairly easy to construct.

Posts are installed in much the same manner as with the fences described in earlier sections. The same attention to detail in post installation is necessary. In addition to posts, picket fences are fastened to horizontal rails, which may either be fastened to notches cut in the posts or nailed to blocks fastened to the posts. In the former case, the notches must be precisely cut in the posts before installing them. To do this, first mark the notches on the posts with a combination square set to the proper depth. Using a handsaw or a portable circular saw, cut down each side of the notch to the proper depth, and then make additional saw cuts down to the depth line. Use a sharp wood chisel to knock out the standing wood pieces and clean up the notch. If you have access to a table or radial arm saw, a much faster and simpler method is to use a dado head in the saw to cut the notches.

You can shape the posts for your picket fence in any of the picket designs shown. Shaping must also be done before the posts

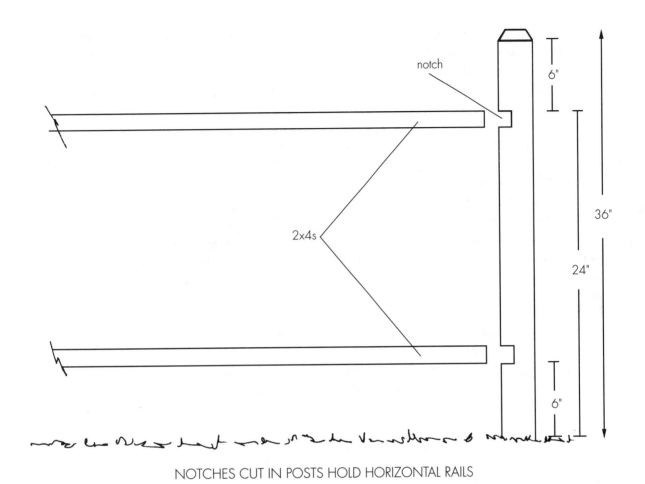

notch

2x4s

6"

36"

24"

6"

NOTCHES CUT IN POSTS HOLD HORIZONTAL RAILS

(1 square = 1")

PATTERNS FOR UPPER ENDS OF PICKETS

are installed in the ground.

Because the rails must fit perfectly between the posts, it's best to install a beginning post solidly in place. Position the second post temporarily, fasten the horizontal support rails to both posts, then anchor the second post. Continue in this manner until all posts are set properly in the fence line. Owing to the weight involved, posts should be spaced no further than 8 feet apart.

With the posts and horizontal support rails installed, adding the pickets is easy. The upper ends of the uprights or pickets are usually shaped in some manner. Several squared drawing designs are shown. Choose the pattern you like and make a grid of 1-inch squares. Count the squares on the original drawing, place dots at each intersection of the pattern and a squared line, and mark the same intersections on your full-sized pattern. Then simply fill in between the dots to finish your pattern. Use a saber or band saw to cut the board ends to the proper shape.

Begin installing the pickets at one end of the rails, but make sure to get the first picket absolutely plumb. Space the pickets evenly and check to be certain they are at the correct height as well. One good method of doing both is to measure and mark each of them on the inside from their bottom edge to the top of the bottom horizontal rail. Position the mark on the top of the bottom rail and fasten the pickets with galvanized 4d nails top and bottom.

A means of achieving even spacing is to make a spacing jig that is the correct width with a support block nailed on its top edge so it can hang on the upper horizontal support rail. To use, merely slide it against the previously installed picket and attach the next picket against it.

PRIVACY FENCING

CREATING A FENCE for privacy and protection is done in much the same manner as the decorative and picket fences. The main difference between the three is the height of privacy fences, which may be as high as 8 feet, although most are 6 feet. Because they offer a lot more surface for the wind to catch, the posts must be very solidly anchored. They must also be absolutely plumb and precisely located.

The top rails in this case are usually fastened down directly on top of the posts. These can be mitered or notched at the corner and butted, diagonally mitered, or notched onto line posts. Bottom rails are held with notches, dadoes, toenailing, or a block on the posts for support.

Once the posts and support rails are in place, the creation of the actual fence style begins. A few designs for different styles of privacy fencing are described on the following pages.

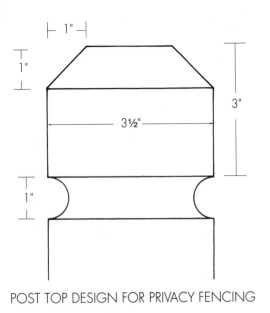

POST TOP DESIGN FOR PRIVACY FENCING

PLAIN BOARD FENCE

This is the simplest and easiest type of fence to build. The boards are nailed in a single layer on one side of the fence to the support framework. The upper ends of the boards can be creatively cut much like picket-style fences.

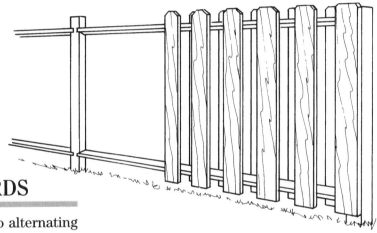

ALTERNATING BOARDS

Individual boards are attached to alternating sides of the fence. This provides some privacy, but also allows air flow.

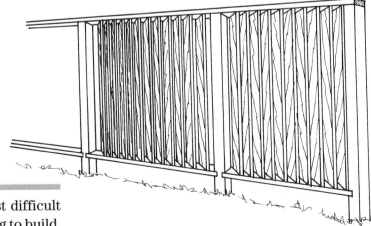

LOUVERED FENCE

A louvered fence is one of the most difficult and time-consuming kinds of fencing to build, but it provides a very interesting and fairly private fence.

ALTERNATING PANELS

This fence has "panels" which are each made from a series of boards all on the same side of the horizontal rails. The sides then alternate from panel to panel.

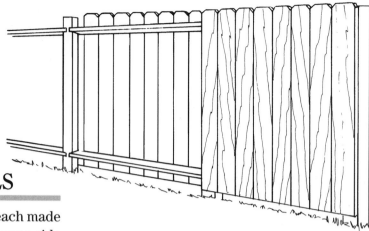

BASKET WEAVE FENCE

Basket weave fencing consists of ½-inch by 6-inch boards woven around a 1×2 nailing strip that is centered between posts. The boards are also alternately nailed to the front and back sides of nailing strips securely nailed to the interior of the posts. Finally a 1×4 cap strip is nailed on top to finish off the fence.

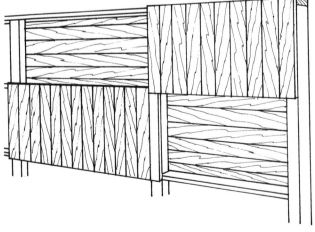

NOVELTY PATTERNS

Boards can also be run in alternating vertical and horizontal patterns between posts or on either side of the posts. Another tactic is dividing the pattern sections in half and creating quarter-patterns on both sides of the fence.

GATES

THERE ARE literally thousands of gate designs. In general, let the purpose of the gate determine the design you choose.

The easiest method of obtaining a gate is to purchase it. A wide variety of sizes, shapes, and types are available including welded steel, bolted aluminum, and wooden with metal braces. The welded-steel gates are the strongest, the aluminum the lightest, and the wooden and steel generally more appropriate to match existing architecture. You can also construct your own all-wood gate using pressure-treated lumber.

Many types of gates can be easily constructed.

WOODEN PASTURE GATE

A wooden gate will last a long time and is more economical than many other styles, although it is heavier than the aluminum and the wood and metal combination gates. Normally wooden board gates are made of 1×6s, although you may prefer to use a material similar to that of your fencing. The gate can be constructed with uprights and bracing on one side or, for more strength, these pieces can be placed on both sides to prevent twisting and warping to one side.

Cut all pieces to the correct size, lay them on a flat surface, and tack-nail them together with one nail in each joint. Use a carpenter's square at the corners to ensure the gate is square, then proceed to nail the pieces solidly together.

With the pieces tack-nailed in place you can finish nailing and assembling the gate in a matter of minutes. If nails protrude on the back side, turn the gate over and clinch them.

WOODEN PASTURE GATE MATERIALS LIST

3   Verticals: 2 × 6 × 37"
4   Horizontals: 1 × 6" × 16'
2   Diagonal braces: 1 × 6" × 9'
Cable, 2 screw eyes, cable clamps, and
    turnbuckle for suspension

This 16-foot pasture gate provides access for large equipment and matches the decorative fencing but is fairly heavy. It requires a cable for additional support.

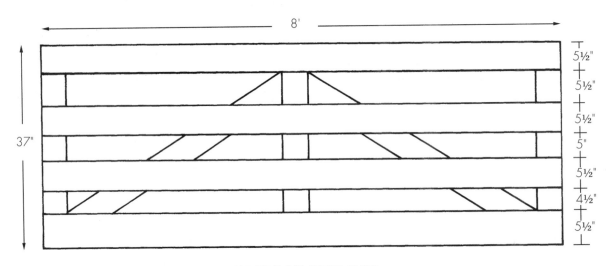

8'

5½"
5½"
5½"
5"
5½"
4½"
5½"

37"

WOODEN PASTURE GATE

PIPE-AND-WIRE GATE

You can make up your own steel pipe gate by either welding ¾- or 1-inch steel plumbing pipe or using T and El plumbing connectors to connect the pipe. Cover the gate with woven wire that is wired to the gate frame on all sides.

DECORATIVE GATE

This decorative gates is assembled in much the same manner as the decorative farm fencing. Gates can be as fancy or simple as the fence itself.

The construction of this decorative gate that matches the farm fencing and fits into the rose arbor on page 154 is typical of most types of gate construction. The construction looks complicated but actually is fairly simple.

Construction

The first step is to create a cardboard pattern of the reversed arch for the top of the gate. Make a pattern that is the same width as the gate, using a compass to establish the line of the arc. Cut the horizontal boards to their correct width and then cut all of the vertical boards to the same length as the longest boards. Another method is to determine each board's approximate length and then cut the boards somewhat long before the final cuts. With all boards cut, temporarily fasten the gate together on a smooth surface with 4d nails driven partially in. Make sure the entire assembly is square. Then lay the cardboard pattern on the top of the gate and trace the arc on the vertical boards. Note that the outside ends also have a reverse arc, which requires tracing out with the compass as well.

Disassemble the gate and trim the upper ends of the vertical boards to the proper shape using a saber or band saw. I used a band saw as it is faster and provides a smoother cut. Once the pieces have all been cut to shape, refasten them to the horizontals with 8d nails clinched on the back, or 1¼-inch wood screws if you prefer to avoid exposed nails on the back of the gate. Fasten the diagonal braces between the upper and lower horizontals. The gate is now ready to hang in place.

Decorative gates can be made to match almost any style of decorative fence.

DECORATIVE GATE MATERIALS LIST

2   Horizontals: 1 × 6 × 36"
2   Outside verticals: 1 × 6 × 50", cut to shape
2   Inside verticals: 1 × 6 × 43", cut to shape
1   Center vertical: 1 × 6 × 40", cut to shape
2   Diagonal braces: 1 × 6 × 48", cut to fit
Decorative gate hardware
Screen door spring

The first step in construction is to temporarily fasten the horizontals and the rough-cut vertical pieces together.

A pattern is created for the decorative top of the gate and transferred to cardboard. The cardboard is then used to mark the gate top for cutting.

The gate pieces are next disassembled and cut along the pattern lines.

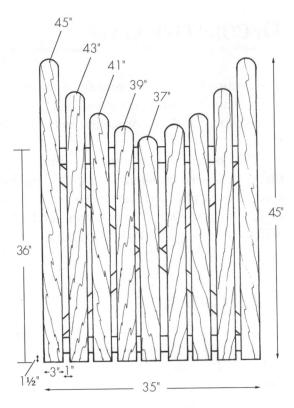

This is another style of decorative gate that includes narrower boards with rounded tops.

The gate is finally permanently reassembled.

64 YARD & GARDEN PROJECTS YOU CAN BUILD YOURSELF

Gates are often hung on L-shaped gate hangers. First, holes are bored for the hangers. They are then turned in place on the posts using a box wrench fitted over the L.

Quite often the upper L is turned down into the hinge strap to prevent the gate from being lifted up off the hangers by livestock. In this case the upper strap is fastened last.

Hanging the Gate

In order for your gate to have a long life, it must be well made as well as properly hung, hinged, and latched. Any number of hinge designs can be used to suit your needs. For heavy gates, L-hangers with steel straps on them are the best choice.

After positioning the gate at the proper height and distance from either side of the opening, you must remember to determine the proper space for the hinging in constructing the gate. The gate should be placed on blocks and propped or held up by another person in a level position until you can determine the exact hinge and latch placement. After marking these locations, you can either put the gate down flat or leave it propped up and fasten the hinges in place. With strap hinges, you can use large lag screws or bolts. If you are attaching L-hinge hangers, install the top L so that it points down. Remove the top hinge strap from the gate, place the gate on the bottom, put the end of the strap up into the down-pointing L

of the hanger, and refasten the hinge strap to the gate.

In the case of long gates, you may need additional support to keep them from sagging and so they can work freely and easily. One method is a cable anchored to a high location

Homemade latches can easily be added to gates for economy or appearance.

(such as an extra-tall fence post) with eye bolts and cable clamps attached to the outer end of the gate. A turnbuckle should be placed in the cable for future tightening and adjustment.

GATE LATCH

Purchased and homemade latches can be installed with wooden gates. You can also use simple hooks to hold the gate in place; some hooks have special keeper bars that prevent them from being rubbed up and off by livestock. A sliding wood latch is quite popular and can easily be operated from either side, which is an important factor with high corral or fence gates.

A sliding wood latch consists of a wooden section sliding between two fence boards. The slider is held in place with wooden "keeper" strips. A dowel fastened to either side of the slider with a wood screw is used to move the bar back and forth to open or close the gate. A small cleat on the back stops the latch from moving backward unless it is lifted up and prevents livestock from accidentally opening the latch.

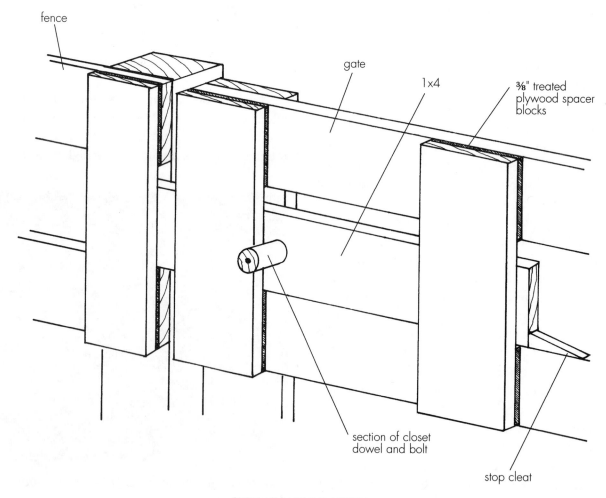

fence

gate

1x4

⅜" treated plywood spacer blocks

section of closet dowel and bolt

stop cleat

SLIDING WOOD LATCH

Index

Page references in *italics* indicate illustrations and photographs.

Other Storey/Garden Way Publishing Books You Will Enjoy

Monte Burch's Pole Building Projects: Over 25 Low-Cost Plans

by Monte Burch

Economical pole building construction saves time, labor, and money. Ideal for first-time builders, it requires no foundation excavation, limited grading, and fewer materials. This detailed book includes plans for rural or suburban locations, from a storage shed or gambrel barn to a garden gazebo or deck-pool surround. 208 pages; 8½" x 11".

How to Build Small Barns & Outbuildings

by Monte Burch

Written specifically for the do-it-yourselfer on a budget, this book takes the mystery out of small-scale construction. Twenty projects are offered with complete plans and step-by-step instructions. Projects include four types of barns, plus plans for a home-office, add-on garage, guest house, workshop, roadside stand, and even an insulated dog house. 288 pages; 8½" x 11".

Building Small Barns, Sheds & Shelters

by Monte Burch

Expand your living, work, and storage areas, with the 20+ projects found in this practical book. Step-by-step instructions and complete plans lead you through the building of small barns, sheds, smoke houses, animal pens, fences, and more. 248 pages; 8½" x 11".

HomeMade: 101 Easy-to-Make Things for Your Garden, Home, or Farm

by Ken Braren & Roger Griffith

Save time and money building dozens of useful items, from wood containers to tool storage units, plant shelves, and outdoor seating. Easy-to-follow instructions and illustrations. 176 pages; 8½" x 11".

Build a Classic Timber-Framed House

by Jack A. Sobon

Architect and builder Jack Sobon clearly explains finding the ideal building site, creating the master plan, hewing and milling timbers, assembling the frame, designing and finishing the interior, and expanding on the plan for your own timber-framed house. 224 pages; 8½″ x 11".

Waterscaping: Plants and Ideas for Natural and Created Water Gardens

by Judy Glattstein

Now you can design and create stunning natural water gardens, or transform wet meadows into beautiful showcases for native water-loving plants. Learn to classify wet areas; select, start, and maintain the best plants; and maintain the best plants, install manufactured water pools, and more. 192 pages; 7⅜" x 9¼".

Stonescaping: A Guide to Using Stone in Your Garden

by Jan Kowalczewski Whitner

Create beautiful effects in your garden by incorporating stone into paths, steps, walls, terraces, ponds, pools, and rock gardens. Twenty basic design plans for a variety of settings, including small urban spaces, large formal gardens, wildlife-attracting areas, and herb gardens. 168 pages; 8½" x 11".

Tips for Carefree Landscapes: Over 500 Sure-Fire Ways to Beautify Your Yard and Garden

by Marianne Binetti

Lazy landscapers rejoice! Here's an invaluable book for everyone who loves an attractive garden, but hates to spend lots of time and energy on it. 168 pages; 6" x 9".

Trellising: How to Grow Climbing Vegetables, Fruits, Flowers, Vines & Trees

by Rhonda Massingham Hart

Grow more — use less space! Clear instructions and photos reveal techniques for building various types of trellises. 160 pages; 6" x 9".

Let It Rot! The Gardener's Guide to Composting

by Stu Campbell

This is the book that has been called the "bible" on the art and science of composting. Author Campbell explains the principles, gives clear instructions for making your own composting "factory," and does it all in a highly readable fashion. 160 pages; 6" x 9".

Easy Garden Design: 12 Simple Steps to Creating Successful Gardens and Landscapes

by Janet Macunovich

Simple, straight-forward approach to garden and landscape design. Techniques are included to design and plant successful gardens, assess site conditions, select the appropriate focal point of the garden, and combine plants to create a workable and attractive garden and landscape in the first year. Plastic comb binding. 164 pages; 8½" x 11".

These books are available at your bookstore, lawn and garden center, or may be ordered directly from Storey Communications, Inc., Department WM, Schoolhouse Road, Pownal, VT 05261.
To order toll-free by phone, call 1-800-441-5700.